A Case for Healing Today

A BIBLICAL, HISTORICAL AND
THEOLOGICAL VIEW OF CHRISTIAN HEALING

Bob Sawvelle

[Scripture quotations are from] New Revised Standard Version Bible, copyright © 1989 National Council of the Churches of Christ in the United States of America. Used by permission. All rights reserved.
ISBN: 1502840820
ISBN 13: 9781502840820
Library of Congress Control Number: 2014920400
CreateSpace Independent Publishing Platform
North Charleston, South Carolina

TABLE OF CONTENTS

TABLE OF CONTENTS

Section Three—Theological Considerations

Dedication

To my loving wife, Carolyn, who has tirelessly worked alongside me to establish our ministry and church in Arizona—thank you for your endless love, friendship, and support to make this book possible.

To my daughter Hannah, who has labored alongside her mother and me to establish our church in Arizona, and to my daughters Lindsay and Ashleigh, for their support of our work here in Arizona. May God richly bless each of you and your families.

ENDORSEMENTS

Dr. Bob Sawvelle, in his new book, *A Case for Healing Today: A Biblical, Historical, and Theological View of Christian Healing*, presents the best and most creative recent scholarship in both theory and practice of this neglected commission of Jesus. This work offers no standard rehash of what you've read before, but serves up many fresh insights into how the healing power of God expresses the truly authentic mission and teaching of Christ himself. *A Case for Healing Today* lays out the very essence of original Christianity; it is a bold challenge to the highly evolved, derivative, and impractical traditional theologies that distract from the clear focus of the core gospel (Rom 1:16).

Jon Mark Ruthven, PhD,
Professor Emeritus, Theology, Regent University;
Doctor of Ministry, Mentor United Theological Seminary

Dr. Bob Sawvelle's book *A Case for Healing Today: A Biblical, Historical, and Theological View of Christian Healing* makes a clear biblical, theological, and church-historical case for the healing ministry today as a normative expression of the gospel and of the ongoing demonstration of the works of Jesus today through the power of the Holy Spirit. This book provides a thirty thousand-foot strategic view of the biblical place of healing in evangelism and church ministry, but it also provides a ground-level, tactical survey of every major biblical passage and theological topic that believers must know to heal the sick and cast out demons effectively today. Combining his background as an engineer and his heart as a church planter, the author uses the tools of careful, thorough research and scholarship to show readers how and why God heals the sick today. This book will convince you that God has always been in the business of taking broken lives and rebuilding, restoring, healing, and delivering them through the power that is released by the forgiveness of the cross and that flows from the resurrected Lord Jesus in Christian healing ministry today.

Gary S. Greig, PhD, adjunct faculty,
United Theological Seminary, Dayton, Ohio;
Vice President of Content, Bible, and Theology, Gospel Light
Publications, Ventura, California; PhD, Near Eastern Languages
and Civilizations, The University of Chicago, 1990

A Case for Healing Today starts with a moving testimony of how an evangelical person, with his spouse, has been touched by the healing power of the Holy Spirit through Randy Clark and has worked as a full-time minister of healing for the transformation of the church and the world. Bob Sawvelle testifies to the power evangelism and love evangelism of Jesus that may change ordinary Christians into extraordinary supernatural Christians with the heart of Jesus.

"Backed by God's power to heal and restore," this book is biblically confirmable, historically verifiable, and theologically authentic. I strongly recommend this book to pastors and laypersons.

Andrew S. Park, PhD, Professor of Theology and Ethics,
United Theological Seminary, Dayton, Ohio

I have had the privilege of traveling with Dr. Bob Sawvelle in Brazil and have witnessed firsthand his passion for the ministry of healing to be restored to the gospel message. As I read through his new book, *A Case for Healing Today: A Biblical, Historical, and Theological View of Christian Healing*, I was struck by the similarity of my own journey into healing. The Biblical, historical, and theological foundation Bob has laid out for the ministry of healing to be fully restored to the church today is crucial for this season of awakening. He has done an outstanding job in combining real scholarship with practical application. In particular, the immense amount of work that has gone into researching the historical record will be a great resource for many pastors and leaders for generations to come. This is the book on healing I wish I had written, and I strongly recommend it.

Steve and Sally Wilson, Senior Pastors, Dayspring, Springfield, Missouri; Members of the Apostolic boards of ANGA and ICLC; Authors of *Keep the Fire Burning* and *Incomplete by Design*

Dr. Bob Sawvelle, in his book, *A Case for Healing Today: A Biblical, Historical, and Theological View of Christian Healing*, has certainly laid a thorough foundation for the relevance of pursuing physical healing. Not only was it valid in the first century, but it is for this century as well. His personal journey of embracing healing will give affirmation to many who have been on that same journey and inspire those who have just began this voyage. His scriptural support clarifies its validity tracing it through the Old and New Testaments. His examination of history corroborates its significance in the proclamation of the Kingdom of God and helps us understand some of the elements which have diminished its significance in some Christian streams. He thoroughly develops the theology using a convergence of thoughts of great scholars and thinkers which includes himself. Sawvelle's content is very weighty and is a tremendous resource and I recommend it for any who are seeking to build on their foundation for ministering to the sick and the oppressed.

Rodney Hogue, DMin,
Author and itinerant minister with over 35 years
of pastoral ministry experience
President of Rodney Hogue Ministries

I have known Bob and Carolyn Sawvelle for more than a decade, and have watched him develop from a fledgling pastor of a small congregation to the solid leader of a thriving revival-minded church that's having vital impact in its community. His book, *A Case for Healing Today,* is a rare combination. Tucson, Arizona's Passion Church, of which Bob is pastor, is a true "laboratory of the Holy Spirit" in which miracles, signs and wonders are weekly happenings. The concepts of this book are not mere theories. They've been hammered out in the crucible of experience. That said, *A Case for Healing* is not merely a compilation of testimonies of God's healing power. It is a thorough examination from a scriptural, theological and historical perspective of God's continued outpouring of love and grace in healing and deliverance. All who aspire to being used by God in supernatural ministry will profit from this work.

Dick Joyce
International conference speaker
President, Global Impact Ministries

FOREWORD

Bob Sawvelle's book, *A Case for Healing Today: A Biblical, Historical, and Theological View of Christian Healing*, is a wealth of information. It is well written. It confirms the fact that the gift of healing never died in the church. This is the kind of book I like to read. It is a serious study of the subject from the Bible, church history, and theology. In each area of study, Bob interacts with biblical scholars, historians, and theologians, showing what their positions actually are and not misrepresenting them as often happens by quoting an earlier belief that was cessationist that they held to, but not telling us that later in life they reversed their position and not only believed in but also practiced healing and deliverance.

A Case for Healing Today is an enlightening read. It is honest scholarship. It is written not from an ivory tower of a seminary, but from the pastoral context of a church planter. Bob was an engineer prior to entering the ministry. His writing reflects his interest in understanding how things really work. I encourage anyone who wants to have a better grounding in the biblical, historical, and theological basis for believing in the continuation of the gifts, especially the gift of healing, to make this book part of his or her library. This book is not milk, it is meat. It is a great introduction for pastors who have questions about the subject of the continuation of the gifts—especially healing and the ministry of deliverance.

You will learn about Martin Luther's belief in healing and his practice of healing. You will learn about John Wesley's belief in and practice of healing. You will learn what modern biblical scholars are writing to champion the cause of healing. You should buy it and have it on your bookshelf or on your e-reader.

Randy Clark, ThD, DMin,
Founder and President of Global Awakening and the Apostolic Network of Global Awakening, Mechanicsburg, Pennsylvania

INTRODUCTION

Through the Old and New Testaments, church history, and Christian theology, all reveal a belief and practice, although weak at times, in the *charisms* or gifts of the Spirit, including healing and deliverance (often referred to as *exorcism*; see "Chapter 7" for further explanation). A theology and kingdom ministry model of power was normal in the early church and should be common for believers today in a twenty-first-century culture. When believed and practiced, the ministry of healing and deliverance, as well as all of the *charisms*, is still operative and effective in our time as it has been in varying degrees throughout church history.

Examining the thread of healing in both the Old and New Testaments, it becomes evident that God is a healer. Christ's atonement was vicarious for both sin and sickness; therefore, salvation and healing are available through the finished work of the cross. The missional work of Jesus, demonstrating the gospel of the kingdom of God in power, was to be replicated by disciples of all ages until his return. Salvation, healing, and deliverance should be a present missional aspect of the church, and when believed and practiced as normative, these gifts aid in the advance of the kingdom of God and church growth.

We see Jesus throughout the Gospels demonstrating the kingdom of God by healing the sick, casting out demons, and performing miracles. The gospel of the kingdom was one of power that healed the sick and delivered the oppressed. After demonstrating this model of ministry to the disciples, Jesus empowered them to do the same: "Then Jesus summoned his twelve disciples and gave them authority over unclean spirits, to cast them out, and to cure every disease and every sickness" (Mt 10:1 NRSV). He commanded them to go, preach, heal, cast out demons, cleanse lepers, and raise the dead as the occasion might demand (cf. Mt 10:7–8; Lk 9:1–2). After his resurrection, he commissioned the disciples to make disciples of all the nations, teaching the people to observe all that they were instructed (cf. Mt 28:18–20). Jesus instructed those disciples to teach others what they had been taught and commanded previously. What were they taught? The disciples were taught how to heal the sick, cast out demons, and proclaim the gospel of the kingdom in power, not just in word.

The gospel of the kingdom of God is a demonstration of the reality that the kingdom of heaven is at hand, as seen through the signs, wonders, and healings that occur. It is more than verbal proclamation; it is backed by God's power to heal and restore. This was the normative Christian ministry for the early church, and Christ intended it to be the common ministry practice for all who would believe and follow him—including the twenty-first-century church. Jesus brought the people into contact with the rule of God's kingdom and, in so doing, gave the disciples authority and opportunity to walk in this same realm and to heal and impart this message to others as they had freely received it—"You received without payment; give without payment" (Mt 10:8 NRSV). The ministries of the twelve, the seventy, and all subsequent disciples who would follow Christ are extensions of the mission and authority of Jesus. The twelve and seventy were trained in how to bring God's kingdom and rule on earth, and were forerunners of a discipleship movement based in the authority and miraculous power that Jesus intended to continue until the *parousia*, his second coming. Christ commanded these disciples to replicate this message and ministry to all who would believe in and follow him.

In the following chapters, I'll present to you a case for the legitimacy of the Christian healing ministry today. We will examine key passages of scripture in both the Old and New Testaments, look at the thread of healing throughout church history, and finally examine a theological basis and framework for the ongoing ministry of healing and deliverance in our day.

Much of the research and sources cited in this book are the result of my doctoral work I completed in 2013. My intention was to capture the dissertation research related to the validity of healing and deliverance ministry in book form for the reader who desires a more involved study of the subject. My sincere prayer is that you will discover, as I have during the past thirty years of my life, that God is a healer, and He desires to use ordinary Christians in extraordinary ways to reveal His love and compassion toward humanity and to reveal His glory and splendor as His power is released.

Chapter 1

JOURNEY INTO THE HEALING MINISTRY

My journey into the healing ministry began as a believer who was frustrated with the lack of "power" I was seeing in my own life and in the body-life of churches my family and I had either attended or were familiar with. From the time that I had accepted Christ as a young man, there was never really a doubt in my mind that God could heal, and oddly enough, I was quite convinced that if God was concerned with every aspect of our lives (after all, Jesus said the very hairs of our head were numbered), then supernatural healing and intervention by God in our lives should be expected. As I read and reread the Gospels and the book of Acts of healing and miracles, I became more and more convinced of this truth that the gifts of the Spirit, including healing and miracles, were still to be expected in our day. Further, I could find no conclusive passage of scripture in the New Testament that indicated healing and deliverance had ceased. Reading the Gospels and the book of Acts created an intense hunger and desire within me to witness God's healing power as a normal part of my Christian faith and in the body-life of the church. Yet I wasn't seeing healing as a reality in my life or in the churches I had attended, which caused me to question at times what seemed to be an obvious revealed truth from scripture.

My formative Christian years were in an evangelical church setting that did not believe healing or the gifts of the Spirit were for today. As a new believer I somehow managed to survive the cessationist teaching prevalent in this environment, although seeds of doubt assailed my mind and heart for the next ten years as to the authenticity of healing ministry. Nonetheless, I found myself in my early thirties with a renewed hunger and desperation for more of God, believing there had to be more power available in the Christian life, yet not seeing healing operate as normative in my life or in the churches my wife and I were acquainted with. I knew many believers and churches that "prayed" for the sick, but rarely did I hear of, or witness myself, healings occur with individuals after they had received prayer. I would continue to read the Gospels, Acts, epistles, and other books, yearning for the authentic kingdom gospel to be made manifest in my time.

I had stacks of books describing the lives of men and women like John Lake, Smith Wigglesworth, Aimee Simple McPherson, and Kathryn Kuhlman, who all moved powerfully in healing ministry during their lifetimes, but it wasn't until I discovered *Power Healing* (and later *Power Evangelism*) by John Wimber, who was one of the founders of the Vineyard movement of churches and was known for healing, that it began to occur to me that there were ordinary Christians in my generation who were experiencing the healing presence and power of God as a normal part of their Christian experience. I discovered *Power Healing* in 1992, about eight years after Wimber first wrote it, and I was hooked—I had to learn and discover more about the gifts of the Spirit and how to operate in the ministry of healing. Little did I know, God was also preparing me for full-time ministry—including several powerful encounters with the Holy Spirit that would soon occur in my life.

In early 1992, my wife and I began to respond to the "nudging" of the Holy Spirit to travel with teams on short-term missions trips. During one of the trips to Haiti in 1993, we were deeply touched by God. It was a powerful trip filled with times of ministering to the poor, praying for the sick, and ministering in churches and to thousands in evangelistic crusades in this impoverished nation—which made a significant impression on both of us. We witnessed hundreds coming to Christ as the power of God moved among the people with healing and deliverance as part of the gospel presentation. It was as if the book of Acts was alive and a new chapter was beginning to unfold in our lives. For the first time in my journey with Christ, I was beginning to observe firsthand what I had been reading about and yearning for. We witnessed the reality that Jesus Christ is the same yesterday, today, and forever (Heb 13:8)!

While on this trip, we were asked by a missions organization to consider serving with them for a season as missionaries in Haiti. After much prayer and counsel, we said yes and headed to Haiti in the spring of 1994 to help serve there. However, we weren't in Haiti but a few months before there was civil unrest between political groups, which created havoc in Haitian society, and in response to the unrest, the United Nations sent troops to help stabilize this impoverished nation. We, along with many other missionaries, were sent home to the States until the situation stabilized there. Little did we know, what seemed like a huge setback and disappointment was about to turn into a divine encounter with the power of the Holy Spirit.

We arrived home to hear about an outpouring of the Holy Spirit in Toronto, Canada, at the Toronto Airport Vineyard Fellowship. As it turned out, we had scheduled a trip from our home base in Florida through several eastern states, finishing in New York State before our scheduled return to Florida. The "buzz" about Toronto had us longing to go and see how God was moving in power through this small church in Canada. We changed our plans and left New York for Toronto for a week before heading back to Florida. It turned out to be a divine encounter and seminal moment in our journey with God.

My wife Carolyn and I were both powerfully touched by the Holy Spirit during our week there in Toronto—God ministered to us at all levels spiritually and emotionally—and the physical manifestations of God's power touching us after receiving prayer were unlike anything we had previously experienced. More significantly, God's loving presence was so tangible—not just during the prayer we received—that His presence became a normal part of our lives from that point forward. During this encounter, a renewed passion for reaching the lost and healing the sick through power evangelism and healing was imparted. Upon our return to Haiti at the end of the summer, a greater release of God's love, compassion, and power to minister and heal the sick was activated in our lives.

A few months later, we were back home in Melbourne, Florida, during the Christmas season, with plans to stay through early January of 1995 before returning to Haiti. During the holiday season, we were told of upcoming meetings in Melbourne with pastor and evangelist Randy Clark. We were thrilled when asked by our pastor to be part of a ministry team that Clark would use during the meetings to pray for the people at the altar. Little did we know that we were about to go to another level in both understanding and impartation for healing.

During the next two weeks of meetings we would participate in, we witnessed some of the most significant healings and miracles we had ever seen—God was moving in power, and people were

coming from around the region to witness a fresh ou
the Holy Spirit.[1] For example, one person Clark prayed for during
these meetings was a pastor suffering from a debilitating neck and
spinal injury as a result of a weight-lifting accident. After roughly
twenty minutes of Clark praying, the pastor was completely healed,
able to move his head and neck without pain, although the vertebrae were previously fused together. This astounded not only the
crowd that night, but later the doctors at Johns Hopkins as the
x-rays revealed the damaged vertebrae were still fused together in
spite of the pastor being pain free and having full range of motion
of his neck!

This one miracle, and the way Clark taught about healing during those meetings, left a lasting impression upon me. Clark taught
about healing in a sound biblical manner, free of hype and manip-
ulation, relying upon the present-day ministry of the Holy Spirit
to accomplish the healing in the name of Christ. I determined
then to learn this model of healing, as it was considerably more
effective than what I had previously learned through Charismatic,
Pentecostal, and Word of Faith training and activations.[2] Later, I
learned Clark's method of healing, and this training, combined
with his anecdotal stories of healing, miracles, and revival, revealed
the connection between healing, deliverance, signs, wonders, and
church growth within me.

---

1 Geoff Waugh, *Revival Fires: History's Mighty Revivals* (Mechanicsburg, PA: The
Apostolic Network of Global Awakening, 2011). Waugh recounts the highlights of this
outpouring of the Holy Spirit in Melbourne, Florida, in January 1995.

2 Randy Clark, *Lighting Fires* (Lake Mary, FL: Creation House, 1998), 41–68. Clark
was impacted as a Baptist pastor by the ministry of John Wimber and the Vineyard
Church movement. Clark later became associated with the Vineyard and began to operate in words of knowledge, healing, and miracles as a normal part of ministry. It was
this Vineyard model and style of ministry that Clark operated in that captivated my
attention.

After completing our season in Haiti, Carolyn and I took positions as mission and youth pastors in Daytona Beach, Florida. My wife and I served in that capacity for nearly two years, growing more in pastoral ministry and leading teams on short-term outreaches and missions trips locally and overseas. The church emphasized a discipleship model of learning how to hear the voice of God and how to operate in revelatory gifts of the Holy Spirit, such as words of knowledge and prophecy. Learning how to function in the revelatory gifts of the Holy Spirit took our ministry to another level of power and effectiveness. However, it was later, with more training from Clark and Global Awakening (GA), that a greater release of the word of knowledge and healing began to operate in our lives. While in Daytona, we learned an inner healing and deliverance model using the Kylstras' Restoring the Foundations (RTF) principles and grew considerably in inner healing and deliverance ministry.[3]

Eventually the Lord relocated our family to Tucson, Arizona, in 2001. Soon after we arrived in Tucson, God began to guide and direct us to establish a church in Tucson that would function as a worship and training center focusing on prayer and worship, ministering to the poor, healing the sick, and delivering the oppressed. Our primary goal was to establish a discipleship model within a local church context that would replicate in other believers the ability to function normatively in the gifts of the Spirit in church settings and evangelistically in the community—as per the missional example and mandate of Jesus. In the spring of 2002, we planted Passion Church (originally known as Tucson Area Christian Fellowship) in our home with six people; twelve years

---

3 Chester and Betsy Kylstra, *An Integrated Approach to Biblical Healing Ministry* (Tonbridge, UK: Sovereign World, 2003), *passim*.

later, Sunday services average approximately two hundred people in a new sanctuary centrally located in Tucson.

Just prior to establishing the church in 2002, I attended a conference in Virginia Beach where I met Pastor Tom Jones, who was affiliated with Clark and GA. Jones shared with conference attendees opportunities to travel with GA teams for missions and ministry outreach. Having previously been impacted by Clark's healing ministry in 1995 in Melbourne, Florida, the opportunity for me to travel with and learn from Clark and GA how to effectively heal the sick and minister deliverance to the demonized was not only compelling, it was to become a God-ordained opportunity that has profoundly impacted my life.

My first trip with Clark, Jones, and GA was to Mozambique in August of 2002 to work alongside Rolland and Heidi Baker, missionaries and founders of Iris Ministries in Mozambique, Africa who oversee thousands of churches, to teach leaders and minister among the poor of that nation. For two weeks, we engaged in ministry to orphans and the poor, training leaders during the day and conducting gospel crusade meetings in the villages in the evening. Healing and deliverance were not only normal in the meetings, but dramatic at times. During one of the meetings, I and a couple of other pastors ministered deliverance to an older woman who was severely demonized due to her involvement with witchcraft. With six Mozambican men holding her, we were able to lovingly lead her through steps to profess her faith in Christ, renounce her involvement with witchcraft, and receive deliverance from the demonic spirits afflicting her. What joy to see this woman stand in her right mind a few minutes later with tears of gratitude streaming down her face after experiencing the freedom that only Christ can give!

Not since our trips and ministry in Haiti had I witnessed God's power to heal, deliver, and transform lives in such dramatic fashion. What we saw in Haiti was powerful, but what I had experienced on this trip to Mozambique was even more dramatic both personally and corporately. Clark believes, and I would concur, that what is taking place in Mozambique with the Bakers is perhaps one of the greatest revivals and people movements taking place in the twenty-first century. Once again, the book of Acts was alive, and it became solidified in my heart both theologically and experientially that we serve a God who is still healing today through ordinary Christians who are completely yielded to Jesus and the power of the Holy Spirit.

Since the trip to Mozambique twelve years ago, I and others from Passion Church have made nearly twenty ministry trips with Clark and GA teams to the nations. Each of these trips has had profound impact, in some cases life changing, for my family and many in our congregation. We've made several powerful trips to Brazil with GA, and all have proved to be missions trips that were really healing and deliverance training sessions for those of us on the teams—as we frequently prayed for twenty or more people each evening during the trips. On two occasions I was invited by Clark to help lead GA teams in India, in which leaders were trained during the day in how to effectively pray for the sick and deliver the oppressed, while in the evening gospel healing crusades were held. Thousands of leaders were trained, and thousands more from the surrounding communities attended the nightly crusade meetings, with hundreds receiving Christ, healing, and deliverance. The result of these trips, along with Carolyn's and my affiliation with Clark and GA as Apostolic Network of Global Awakening (ANGA) ministers and network church members, has aided significantly in the creation of a supernatural church culture where healing and deliverance ministry is normal and expected in Passion Church body-life.

In 2007 and 2008, we hosted Clark and GA in Tucson for two powerful healing schools, which not only saw many healed in the meetings, but also trained several hundred participants in healing and deliverance ministry in our community. In the 2007 healing school, there was a significant healing involving a young woman who was diagnosed with schizophrenia soon after going to college. The illness was debilitating, causing her to be withdrawn, isolated, and unable to function socially or in a work environment. Her healing was a breakthrough in the area of mental illness for Clark and GA associates.[4] Today, as a result of the GA training many believers in our community received during these schools, as well as additional healing rooms training in our area, there are now presently several churches that have formed healing teams and healing rooms in Tucson.[5]

Our church has become known as a place in Tucson where healing, miracles, and deliverance are common. We frequently

---

4 Bill Johnson and Randy Clark, *Healing Unplugged* (Bloomington, MN: Chosen Books, 2012), 126. Clark writes of the healing: "Everything else was falling, but we still had this Goliath, and it was schizophrenia. In Tucson, Arizona, though, we saw a young woman who was in the psych ward with schizophrenia 180 days a year. She could not even speak in sentences. She was marvelously healed, kind of a sovereign healing in a way. God had spoken some things to her dad. And the guy who prayed for her just said, 'I bless you in Jesus' name.' Then she heard the Lord tell her to anoint herself with oil. She went home and anointed herself with flaxseed oil, then she lay trembling on the floor all night. The next morning, she was normal." I happened to be the person who prayed a simple prayer of blessing over her. She occasionally attends our church, and my wife and I have kept in contact with her and her family over the past few years—she continues to function normally in social settings, showing a truly remarkable healing.

5 For more on the global impact of Global Awakening (GA), see Candy Gunther Brown, *Testing Prayer: Science and Healing* (Cambridge, MA: Harvard University Press, 2012), 21–63. A particularly helpful observation is on page 38: "The Apostolic Network of Global Awakening is one of a number of transnational, cross-cultural, relational, and institutional networks whose divine healing practices are contributing to the global expansion of Christianity."

have special healing services (although we pray for the sick during every service) and are involved in outreach where healing the sick and delivering others from demonic oppression are common in our community. We train our church members in the GA five-step prayer model, how to receive words of knowledge, and how to minister deliverance. We train and encourage believers to not only minister to others within the church setting, but to be evangelistically focused using these techniques as tools for evangelism. As you will see in this book, I felt so strongly about the link between power evangelism and church growth that my doctoral thesis and project centered on what I call Encounter Evangelism.[6]

One of the men in our church, Rick, was powerfully impacted by training he received in healing and evangelism ministry a couple of years ago. Here is his testimony right after receiving the training: Rick was in Fry's supermarket looking at soup. New to the gifts of the Spirit and a lifestyle of Encounter Evangelism, he and an unsuspecting shopper were about to have a supernatural encounter with God's love and power in the canned food aisle'. He heard the Lord say to him, "Put the soup down and pray for the woman behind you." A little stunned, he turned around and saw a woman trying to reach a high can on the opposing shelf. He asked if he could help her reach the can, and she responded "Yes," grateful for his assistance. He then took a chance and asked if he could pray for her arm to be healed, and once again she said yes. Apparently, she had a severe problem in her arm that prevented her from lifting the arm very high, coupled with an extreme amount of pain in the arm. He prayed a simple prayer for her, commanding the pain to leave and mobility to return to her arm in the name of Jesus, and then told her to try to move it—to do

---

6 My doctoral thesis is titled "Encounter Evangelism: Utilizing the Charisms of the Holy Spirit to Aid in Evangelism and Church Growth."

something with it she could not before. She briefly tried to move the arm, but had little improvement. She then thanked him for his help in getting the can off the shelf and exclaimed as she walked away, "Well, at least someone prayed!"

A few minutes later, Rick was in the produce section looking at tomatoes. This same woman suddenly came rushing over toward him shouting in a loud voice, "What did you do to me? My arm is totally healed!" She was now able to lift her arm over her head with complete mobility and pain free. This created a stir among the other shoppers, and soon a small crowd gathered around Rick in the produce section. One of the guys in the crowd asked, "Can you pray for my knee?" Rick agreed and prayed for the man's knee, and the man received healing—the pain left, and he had movement again in his knee that he did not have before receiving prayer. Another man asked for prayer and received prayer for his elbow, with the pain leaving and mobility returning to the arm and elbow. After praying for these two men, Rick finished shopping and made his way to the checkout counter, where the manager asked him, "What was going on in my produce department?" Rick rather cautiously explained about the woman and the two men receiving prayer for healing and how God had healed all three of them. The manager then said, "Well, can you pray for me too?" Rick proceeded to pray for a condition the manager had, and then the manager asked how he could help the church with food donations!

Rick shared his experience with the Encounter Evangelism class, and again at the Passion Church service the following Sunday: "I have never done anything like this before, but through the training received in the class and what I just saw God do, I now have the confidence to pray for people for healing and to share Christ with them in public." Rick continues to use his new Encounter Evangelism skills to minister to people he comes in contact with while in public. Perhaps what is most interesting in Rick's case is the fact that he is a quiet, soft-spoken person—one you would not consider gregarious or a "natural evangelist." He is simply a person who has learned how to hear God's voice and obey the leading of the Holy Spirit. He is now confident God can use him as a vessel through which God's love and healing power can flow to minister to others.

My journey into healing over the years, while slow and frustrating at first, has overall been amazing. I'm so thankful that God opened my eyes to the truth of healing and deliverance for today and gave me many opportunities to receive teaching and training in this essential area of Christian ministry. I'm grateful for the pioneers of modern healing ministry, men such as Wimber and Clark—and countless others—who have paid the price to learn how to hear God's voice, pray effectively for the sick, and to persist despite ridicule and disdain by many both within and outside of the church. I'm even more grateful that Wimber, Clark, and others learned the value of replicating this model of kingdom discipleship, which includes healing and deliverance ministry, in the lives of others. Their diligence in training others has created a movement in many churches of ordinary believers praying effectively for others to be healed. As a result of the training I have received in this area of ministry, I and many others in our church have now witnessed many significant healings, both abroad and at Passion Church over the last several years, and I've wondered, Where would some of these people be today if we hadn't believed the case for healing today and learned and put into practice the methods of healing ministry we've gleaned over the years?

Case in point, earlier this year, our church office received a phone call from a man who had a close friend who was in a coma at St. Joseph's Hospital in Tucson. He had heard about some of the healings that had occurred at our church and wondered if a couple of men could go to the hospital to pray for his friend Anthony. My wife arranged for a couple of our men to go and pray with Anthony for his healing. It turns out that Anthony had been in the hospital for weeks due to a severe heart condition and had slipped into a coma, and the doctors had begun to prepare the family for the possibility of his death—in fact, they were getting ready to send him to hospice because there was nothing more they could do. These men, over a period of a few weeks, went to his hospital room to pray for him, and soon there was significant improvement. Eventually after several weeks of consistent prayer ministry, Anthony awoke from the coma and was eventually able to get out of bed and walk, leave the hospital, and return to a normal lifestyle—he was miraculously healed! The doctors and nurses were amazed; all who knew of Anthony's condition called it a miracle. Anthony and his wife now attend our church—we serve an amazing God who still heals today through ordinary believers who know their authority in Christ. Had these humble servants not gone and persisted in prayer for weeks, the story probably would have turned out differently for Anthony.

Recently, Sue, who attends our church, shared with our congregation how her stage-four pancreatic cancer has dramatically decreased since attending our church and receiving prayer. Of the fifteen tumors she was diagnosed with, only two remain, and they have shrunk significantly. Additionally, her pathogen numbers have improved steadily in the last couple of months—she attributes the progressive healing to the prayer she has received, combined with the medical treatment she has also been receiving. Her closing comments: "I'm so thankful for this church and the faithful prayers by so many."

It's not about our church as much as it is about ordinary believers who know what Christ has commissioned them to do and being faithful in demonstrating the Gospel through healing, deliverance, and other gifts of the Spirit. While we may never know how much effect medical treatment has also had on Sue's cancer, we do know that her condition was serious, if not fatal in most cases, and she is now seeing remarkable improvement—to that we give God glory and are thankful for the attending doctors and medical treatments she is receiving. She is vibrant and radiating God's love and peace through the midst of a challenging health situation, and prayer for healing has certainly helped her condition and her attitude. Christians who understand the Great Commission from a kingdom perspective, which includes healing and deliverance ministry, frequently observe dramatic healings and miracles as they pray for others, as well as more effectiveness in evangelism and church growth.[7]

I'm convinced that *A Case for Healing Today* is biblically accurate, historically representative, and theologically sound. I encourage you to read with an open heart to believe and learn the truth behind the validity of the Christian healing ministry for today. May your journey into healing ministry be rich and rewarding, as many today are in need of God's love and power through ordinary people like you and me.

---

7 Brown, *Testing Prayer*, 27. According to Brown, "ANGA-bridged networks—though not coterminous with global pentecostalism—exemplify the multidirectional, global patterns of cultural exchange through which healing prayer feeds Pentecostal growth." Encountering God through healing prayer or other *charisms* of the Spirit has continued to be an effective means of evangelism since Christ instituted this missional model.

Section 1

BIBLICAL
CONSIDERATIONS

Chapter 2

THE LORD WHO HEALS

EXODUS 15:22–27

In this passage, the children of Israel have just been delivered from the cruel bondage of Pharaoh and the Egyptians. God miraculously brings the Israelites through the parted waters of the Red Sea, and after great celebration, they realize they are in a wilderness place with no water and are thirsty. This short narrative provides a picture of need and barrenness and yet God's power to heal and provide, contrasted by the bitter water of Marah and the oasis at Elim.

The children of Israel have wandered three days in the wilderness where they have found no water. They then come to the bitter waters of Marah, and it is here, in this setting of desert wilderness, that they complain to Moses, asking him, "What shall we drink?" Moses cries out to God, and God shows him a piece of wood (some translations say tree) that he throws into the water, and the water becomes sweet. The narrative then explains, "There the Lord made for them a statute and an ordinance and there he put them to the test" (Ex 15:25 NRSV).

What follows is a conditional covenant promise that God makes to the people. God promises, "If you will listen carefully to the voice of the Lord your God, and do what is right in his sight, and give heed to his commandments and keep all his statutes, I will not bring upon you any of the diseases that I brought upon the Egyptians; for I am the Lord who heals you" (Ex 15:26 NRSV). God hereby gives a promise of protection and healing to the Israelites as contrasted to the plagues inflicted upon the Egyptians. God expresses the desire for healing and wholeness of the nation and individual. This theme of healing is a thread that now weaves through the entirety of scripture, becoming normative in both the Old and New Testaments. God gives an announcement, stating, "I am the Lord who heals you," or it could be translated, "I am the Lord, your doctor." In essence, the story in Exodus of the Israelites' struggle with Egypt and subsequent emancipation can be understood as the nation's healing and deliverance by God.[1]

Walter Brueggemann, professor emeritus of Old Testament at Columbia and influential Protestant Old Testament scholar and theologian, in the book *I Am the Lord Who Heals You*, explains this passage primarily as God's promise to protect and heal the Israelites from systemic problems due to societal injustice and dysfunction. God, as the doctor of humanity, promises to heal societal systemic illnesses. Brueggemann states, "If, however, we accept YHWH as a 'systems doctor,' then we may understand the 'diseases of Egypt' as 'systemic maladies' that come with the territory of large socio-economic systems that have no capacity for human compassion."[2]

---

1 Walter Brueggemann, "Healing and its Opponents (Exodus 15:19–26; Mark 3:1–6)," in *I Am the Lord Who Heals You* (Nashville, TN: Abingdon Press, 2004), 2.

2 Ibid., 3.

He continues his discussion by stating that good medical doctors are going to encourage adherence to healthy lifestyles for their patients as conditions for maintaining optimal health and healing.[3]

In like manner, God is prescribing the conditions for good health for the children of Israel as those of listening to God's voice and obeying God's commands. Michael L. Brown, president and professor of practical theology at Fellowship for International Revival and Evangelism School of Ministry and author of *Israel's Divine Healer*, states,

> The text indicates that covenantal obedience would bring about supernatural blessings of health—i.e., more than just reaping the rewards of "clean," godly living—while breech of covenant would be (supernaturally) disastrous....It seems best to view Yahweh's function as "Healer"...whose role was to both heal and keep well. Thus, as Healer, he made the waters of Marah drinkable; in the future, if Israel obeyed, he would keep them free from sickness. If they encountered sickness, barrenness, infertility (physical or agricultural), or undrinkable water, he would be their *rope* and make these wrong conditions right.[4]

Perhaps God is alluding to the Ten Commandments that will later be given at Mt. Sinai in Ex 20. Again, God's promise is that "if you will listen...and do what is right...give heed...keep all his statutes...then I will..." God promises to provide a societal and individual level of protection and healing to those who hear and obey God's voice. Brueggemann states, "This God works not only by one-on-one remedies but also by facing the systems of death and

---

3 Brueggemann, "Healing and its Opponents," 3–4.

4 Michael L. Brown, *Israel's Divine Healer* (Grand Rapids, MI: Zondervan Publishing House, 1995), 77. Cf. Brown 72–78 for thorough discussion of this topic.

by robbing them of authority. It is the same God who is present in Jesus of Nazareth."[5]

In the context of the Ex 15 narrative, Brueggemann's view of God as healer at a societal level is perhaps an accurate view of the passage considering the abuse the children of Israel suffered as a whole under the Egyptians, the plagues that afflicted Egypt, and God's desire to bring the Israelites into close relationship with Him. However, Brueggemann also recognizes the healing attributes of God on an individual level. One could easily conclude that if God is concerned about the healing of a nation, then God would desire the healing of individuals within a nation as well.

In Ex 15:25, God puts the people to a test, in two respects. First, will they trust God through Moses as the bitter waters are made sweet? And second, will they listen to God's voice and completely obey God as their covenant protector and healer? The healing of the bitter waters was to be a sign to the people, a revelation of God's healing virtue. God demonstrated this revelation to the people in healing the waters and then gave them the interpretation of what that miracle represented in verse 26. Through this sign, God was proving not only the ability and power to heal, but also the willingness to heal the Israelites (and humanity) of all their spiritual and natural diseases. When considered in light of God's character, it can be believed that what God did in this instance is also intended as a demonstration to humanity that God will do it forever. God is eternally identical and consistent in actions and principles. Therefore, when God has acted one way before, it can be assumed that God will act again in a similar manner. If God promised the children of Israel to heal, it can be concluded that God has established a spiritual principle and precedent now for continued healing.

---

5 Brueggemann, "Healing and its Opponents," 4.

Henry Donald Maurice Spence-Jones, a Hebrew scholar and lecturer in the last decades of the nineteenth century and the start of the twentieth century, explains of this passage, "The lesson God would have them learn from the incident was—'I am Jehovah that healeth thee.'" Spence-Jones continues by stating that "As Jehovah, God is the Being of exhaustless resource. As Jehovah, he is the Being eternally identical with himself—self-consistent in all his ways of acting; so that from any one of his actions, if the principle of it can but be clearly apprehended, we are safe in inferring what he always will do."[6]

Encapsulated in this overarching promise of protection and healing for the nation is God's covenant promise of healing for the individual. Revealed in this promise is an aspect of God's nature, that of healer, Jehovah Rapha, "the Lord who heals you." Iain D. Campbell, an adjunct professor of church history at Westminster Theological Seminary, explains in his commentary *Opening Up Exodus* that God's promise to the Israelites is that as they listen and obey, He will not allow them to be afflicted with diseases that plagued the Egyptians. The challenge lies in walking in total obedience and consecration to God.[7] The sweetening of the waters was proof and a pledge of God's character and power as Jehovah the Healer—a demonstration that God would be a God of health to them as they obeyed and walked faithfully with God.[8]

As noted earlier, the phrase in Ex 15:26 "the Lord who heals you" could be translated "I am the Lord, your doctor." James Strong, a nineteenth-century American Methodist Biblical scholar and educator, and the creator of the widely used *Strong's*

---

6 H. D. M. Spence-Jones, ed., *Exodus*, The Pulpit Commentary, vol. 2 (London: Funk & Wagnalls Company, 1909), 23–24.

7 Iain D. Campbell, *Opening Up Exodus* (Leominster, UK: Day One Publications, 2006), 63–65.

8 Spence-Jones, *Exodus*, 23–24.

Concordance, explains that the English word *heal* is translated from the Hebrew word *rāpā',* which primarily means to mend, to cure, to heal, to make whole, and to repair.[9] Wilhelm Gesenius and Samuel Prideaux Tregelles, nineteenth-century Hebrew scholars and authors of *Gesenius' Hebrew and Chaldee Lexicon to the Old Testament Scriptures,* explain that within the word *rāpā'* is the idea of someone sewing rapidly, such as a cobbler, or a physician sewing together a wound.[10] Hebrew scholar William White writes in the *Theological Wordbook of the Old Testament* that usually a human

---

9 James Strong, *A Concise Dictionary of the Words in the Greek Testament and the Hebrew Bible,* vol. 2 (Bellingham, WA: Logos Research Systems, 2009), 110. Strong states, "7495 רָפָא râphâ', *raw-faw';* or רָפָה râphâh, *raw-faw';* a prim. root; prop. to *mend* (by stitching), i.e. (fig.) to *cure:*—cure (cause to) heal, physician, repair, × thoroughly, make whole."

10 Wilhelm Gesenius and Samuel Prideaux Tregelles, *Gesenius' Hebrew and Chaldee Lexicon to the Old Testament Scriptures* (Bellingham, WA: Logos Research Systems, 2003), 775–76. Gesenius and Tregelles state, "1)—רָפָא) prop. to sew together, to mend. (Arab. رفا, Æth. ረፈየ፡ id. To this answers the Gr. ῥάπτω. These roots spring from the primary and onomatopoet. stock רף, which has the sense of seizing and plucking, *rapiendi* and *carpendi,* Germ. *raffen, rupfen* (kindred רוב *raufen*), *rauben,* compare גָּרַף, הָרַף, טָרַף. This root imitates the sound of a person sewing rapidly.) See Niphal and Piel No. 1. Hence— (2) *to heal,* pr. a wound, a wounded person (which is done by sewing up the wound), Is 19:22; 30:26; Job 5:18; Eccl 3:3; compare Ps 60:4; hence a sick person (compare Gr. ἀκεῖσθαι, i.e., *sarcire* and *sanare,* and Luther's joke, who calls the physicians, *unferes Herrn Gottes Flicker,* the cobblers of our Lord God); with an acc. of pers. Gn 20:17; Ps 60:4; with a dat. of pers. Nm 12:13; 2 Kgs 20:5. Part. רֹפֵא a doctor, Gn 50:2; 2 Chr 16:12. Impers. Is 6:10, וְרָפָא לוֹ 'and (lest) there be healing done to them,' lest they recover."

subject is the object of the healing, but other objects can be the recipients of healing as well.[11]

From these definitions, we find that the primary meaning of the word *rāpā'* is to mend, cure, repair, and make whole, cause to heal, or cause to heal by a physician. The imagery is that of God stitching together, like a physician sewing together a wound, for the purpose of mending and making the person whole. The initial occurrence of the word *rāpā'* is in Gn 20:17, where Abraham was directed by God to pray for Abimelech and his household in order that they would be healed. God answers the prayer and heals Abimelech of a plague and the women of bareness; thus, curing, mending, and wholeness were the results of God answering prayer.

In Ex 15:26, God introduces to humanity the promise to heal, whether on an individual basis or at a societal level, and Jewish people through the centuries have believed this promise. God declares, "I am Yahweh, the one who heals you." As mentioned, the participle "who heals you" could be translated "your healer"

---

11 William White, *Theological Wordbook of the Old Testament,* ed. R. Laird Harris, Gleason L. Archer, Jr., and Bruce K. Waltke (Chicago: Moody Press, 1999), 857. White states, "2196 רָפָא (*rāpā'*) *heal, make healthful.* This is a purely Hebrew root which appears over sixty times in the ot and is cognate only to a few later forms in Afro-Semitic dialects. The meaning is straightforward in virtually all passages. In the initial occurrence (Gn 20:17) in which God heals Abimelech, the Qal stem is employed. The root is also used of human healing, as a substantive, 'physician' (Gn 50:2). *rāpā'* is also used of the healing and forgiveness of Gentile nations (Is 19:22; 57:18). In the Piel and Hithpael stems the causative aspect is foremost (I Kgs 18:30), 'He healed (repaired) the altar.' However, a human subject is generally the object of the healing (Ex 21:19), 'He shall cause him to be thoroughly healed.' The Hithpael has the passive mood characteristic of the stem (II Kgs 8:29; 9:15), 'In order that he could be healed.' The other occurrence of the Hithpael is II Chr 22:6. Possibly the most significant usage is in the Ni-phal stem (I Sam 6:3), 'Then you shall be healed;' (Dt 28:27), 'of which you cannot be healed.' The stem is also used for the restoration of objects (II Kgs 2:22); the turning of salt water into fresh (Jer 19:11). The themes of healing and restoration as connotations of *rāpā'* are combined in the usage of Isa 53:5, 'With his stripes we are healed.' In many of the occurrences, it is God who causes healing or afflicts with disease or catastrophes which cannot be healed but by divine intervention."

or "your doctor."[12] Brueggemann continues, "Thus there is intro-
duced into Israel's rhetoric God's concern for the therapeutic,
which stands in complete contrast to the Egyptian powers who
generate disease."[13] According to Craig S. Keener, professor of New
Testament at Asbury Theological Seminary, and author of *Miracles*,
"Jewish people, after all, attributed healing to the one true God
(Ex 15:26), in whom Jesus believed, and prayed to God regularly
for healing Israel's sicknesses."[14] Morton Kelsey, a twentieth-century Episcopal priest, counselor and teacher at Notre Dame, and
author of *Healing and Christianity*, writes that in the time of Jesus,
there were many Jewish healers that used Ex 15:26 to elicit God to
heal, despite the disapproval of the rabbis.[15] According to Kelsey,
"Still, people sought some relief from their sufferings, and so a
form was used in which the healer whispered words adapted from
Ex 15:26....The main schools of Judaism considered the practice
involved here akin to sorcery and magic and forbade it, but the
Talmud attests to its use."[16]

Throughout the Old Testament, the examples of God's healing and miracle power are evident, confirming God's covenant
nature to heal. As previously mentioned, we read of God healing
Abimelech and his household through the prayer of Abraham in
Gn 20. We also read of the healing of Miriam's leprosy in Nm 12 as
Moses prays for her, the children of Israel receiving healing in Nm
21 as they look upon the bronze serpent, Naaman being healed of

---

12 Walter Brueggemann, "The Book of Exodus: Introduction, Commentary, and
Reflections," *The New Interpreter's Bible*, vol. 1 (Nashville, TN: Abingdon Press, 1994),
808.

13 Ibid.

14 Craig S. Keener, *Miracles: The Credibility of the New Testament Accounts* (Grand
Rapids, MI: Baker Academic, 2011), 1:58.

15 Morton Kelsey, *Healing and Christianity: A Classic Study* (Minneapolis, MN:
Augsburg Fortress, 1995), 32.

16 Ibid.

leprosy as he dips in the Jordan following the command of Elisha in 2 Kgs 5, and King Hezekiah being healed by God through medical treatment in 2 Kgs 20. Even the dead are raised by Elijah and Elisha in 1 Kgs 17 and 2 Kgs 4, respectively.

The theme is continued throughout the book of Psalms. Kelsey comments on this theme of God as healer in the Psalms, "In Ps 103 Yahweh is blessed for healing diseases and Ps 91 tells how God protects from all plague. Similar confidence of Yahweh as healer of mind and body and social and political condition is found in Pss 41, 46, 62, 74, 116, 121, and 147."[17] These, and other cases, are examples of God's healing and miraculous power as promised by God in Ex 15:26. The Old Testament also points to a day when a great prophet would rise among the people continuing a miraculous ministry similar to that of Moses.

The narrative in Dt 18:15–22 states that God will raise up a prophet, like Moses, who will be a spokesperson for God and of the Torah. According to Michael D. Coogan, who is a lecturer on Hebrew Bible/Old Testament at Harvard Divinity School, professor emeritus of Religious Studies at Stonehill College, and editor of *The New Oxford Annotated Bible: New Revised Standard Version with Apocrypha*, Moses was the "paradigmatic prophet" of the Old Testament.[18] When we examine the life of Moses carefully, we see not only one who communicates the divine oracles of God to the people, but one who performs miracles in the name of Yahweh. In reference to Jesus Christ, Brad H. Young, a professor of Biblical Literature in Judeao Christian Studies at Oral Roberts University, and author of *Jesus the Jewish Theologian*, writes, "The Jews of the

---

17 Kelsey, *Healing and Christianity*, 34.

18 Michael D. Coogan, ed., *The New Oxford Annotated Bible: New Revised Standard Version with Apocrypha*, 4th ed. (New York: Oxford University Press, 2010), 280. Cf. Dt 18:15–22n.

period thought 'the prophet' would be like Moses (Dt 18:18)...
[who] was interpreted as referring to the coming messiah."[19]

M. Eugene Boring, professor emeritus of New Testament at
Brite Divinity School, and author of books on biblical scholarship,
describes the eschatological nature of the prophet like Moses, who
was "expected to renew the Mosaic miracles."[20] Passages such as Is
53:5–6 were understood in Judaism to describe the eschatological
season of miracles.[21] The early church, with its Jewish roots, viewed
Christ as the fulfillment of these prophecies, due to the "messianic power" visibly present in him. According to Boring, "Miracle
stories make the presence and power of the kingdom visible. They
portray Jesus in such a way that messianic power is visibly present
in him. They are stories of the coming of the kingdom and the
messianic age, not stories of Jesus as a man with great power. They
are thus, like all talk of the kingdom of God and the coming of the
Messiah, theocentric rather than Jesu-centric."[22]

19 Brad H. Young, *Jesus the Jewish Theologian* (Peabody, MA: Hendrickson
Publishers, 1995), 198.

20 M. Eugene Boring, "The Gospel of Matthew: Introduction, Commentary, and
Reflections," in *The New Interpreter's Bible*, vol. 8 (Nashville, TN: Abingdon Press, 1995),
249.

21 Ibid.

22 Ibid.

Chapter 3

HEALING IN THE ATONEMENT

ISAIAH 53:4–5

In Is 52 and 53, we begin to view the mission of this prophet and what he will endure as the suffering servant to fulfill this mission. This is the fourth and final servant song in Isaiah, and according to Talmudic tradition, the servant in Is 52:13–53:12 is Moses; however, early Christian tradition identifies the servant with Jesus (Acts 8:32–35).[1] Others have argued that the servant is Israel, Jeremiah, King Josiah, and King Jehoiachin.[2] However, Kenneth D. Litwak, an adjunct professor of New Testament studies at Azusa Pacific University and Asbury Seminary, writes, "The Servant then in Is 52:13–53:12 is an individual whose mission

---

1 Coogan, *New Oxford Annotated Bible*, 1039. Cf. Is 52:13–53:12n.

2 Ibid; cf. Kenneth D. Litwak, "The Use of Quotations from Isaiah 52:13–53:12 in the New Testament," *Journal of the Evangelical Theological Society* 26, no. 4 (December 1, 1983): 385.

carries messianic overtones. Understanding the passage in this way allowed the Church to apply it readily to Jesus."[3]

Mt 8:16–17 intentionally identifies Jesus to the servant in Is 53. Describing the type and magnitude of the healings occurring in Capernaum in verse 16, Matthew quickly adds in verse 17, "This was to fulfill what had been spoken through the prophet Isaiah; 'He took our infirmities and bore our diseases'" (NRSV). It seems quite apparent that the writer of Matthew is stressing to his readers that Jesus is indeed the promised Messiah and great prophet mentioned in Talmudic tradition. Jesus, functioning as healer, fulfills the messianic prophecy of Is 53:4, bearing our infirmities and carrying our diseases. As Donald Senior, professor of New Testament Studies and president of Catholic Theological Union, writes in *The Gospel of Matthew, Interpreting Biblical Texts*, "It is significant that Matthew envelops Jesus as healer in the mantle of Isaiah's Suffering Servant. Through his healings the Matthean Jesus not only takes away the sufferings of God's people but bears them himself."[4]

In Lk 22:37, Jesus is identified with the transgressors of Is 53:12: "For I tell you, this scripture must be fulfilled in me, 'And he was counted among the lawless'; and indeed what is written about me is being fulfilled" (NRSV). According to Luke, Jesus associates himself and the sufferings awaiting him at the cross with the suffering servant passage of Is 52:13–53:12.

In Acts 8:30–35, Philip encounters the Ethiopian eunuch reading Is 53. This passage provides a compelling relationship between the suffering servant in Isaiah and the ministry of Jesus. As Philip explains the Isaiah passage to the eunuch, answering his questions

---

3 Litwak, "Use of Quotations from Isaiah," 386.

4 Donald Senior, *The Gospel of Matthew, Interpreting Biblical Texts* (Nashville, TN: Abingdon Press, 1997), 112–113.

concerning the suffering servant and explaining that he is Jesus (verse 35), he provides a convincing case for both the early and present-day church that the Is 53 servant is in fact Jesus.

The writer of 1 Pt 2:24 also unites Is 53 to the Christological mission of Jesus: "He himself bore our sins in his body on the cross, so that, free from sins, we might live for righteousness; by his wounds you have been healed" (1 Pt 2:24 NRSV). While writing to slaves who will endure additional suffering, Peter links Christ and his suffering to that of the suffering servant in Is 53. Boring states, "The passage pictures Christ as the suffering servant of Is 53. The details and vocabulary do not come from historical memory of what happened during the trial and crucifixion of Jesus, nor from the author's adoption of Pauline theology, but from the Scripture."[5] David L. Bartlett, professor emeritus of Christian Communication at Yale Divinity School and professor emeritus of New Testament at Columbia Theological Seminary, writes of this passage in *The New Interpreter's Bible* commentary, "And there is yet another image of the salvation worked in Christ in the citation from Is 53:5 in vs. 24. Now Jesus is the wounded surgeon whose wounds heal the wounded believers."[6]

It is apparent from a Christian perspective that Is 53:4–5 not only unites this passage to the Christological mission of Jesus, but also describes in detail what Christ, the suffering servant, will carry and endure for others in fulfilling his mission: "Surely he has borne our infirmities and carried our diseases; yet we accounted him stricken, struck down by God, and afflicted. But he was wounded for our transgressions, crushed for our iniquities;

---

5 M. Eugene Boring, "1 Peter," in *Abingdon New Testament Commentaries* (Nashville, TN: Abingdon Press, 1999), 120.

6 David L. Bartlett, "The First Letter of Peter: Introduction, Commentary, and Reflections," in *The New Interpreter's Bible*, vol. 12 (Nashville, TN: Abingdon Press, 1998), 283.

upon him was the punishment that made us whole, and by his bruises we are healed" (Is 53:4–5 NRSV). It is important to note that the English word *healed* is the same Hebrew word *rāpā'* previously discussed in the exegesis of Ex 15:26. According to William White, "The themes of healing and restoration as connotations of *rāpā'* are combined in the usage of Is 53:5, 'With his stripes we are healed.'"[7] The use of the word *rāpā'* in this passage clearly implies healing.

Is 53:4–5 describes the servant bearing or carrying our infirmities and diseases, as well as being bruised or wounded for our healing. The Hebrew for infirmities is *ḥŏlî* (*choli*), which is predominately translated "sickness, disease, illness, malady, sickbed, affliction, and infirmity" by both Thomas and Brown-Driver-Briggs.[8] According to Francis Brown, Samuel Rolles Driver, and Charles Augustus Briggs, editors of *A Hebrew and English Lexicon of the Old Testament*, which is a standard reference for Biblical Hebrew and Aramaic, the word *diseases* in Is 53:4 is translated from the Hebrew word *makob* or *makobah*, primarily meaning pain, physical and

---

7 White, *Theological Wordbook*, 857.

8 Robert L. Thomas, *New American Standard Hebrew-Aramaic and Greek Dictionaries* (Anaheim, CA: Foundation Publications, 1998), 2483. Thomas states, "2483.חֳלִי choli (318b); from 2470a; *sickness:*—affliction(1), disease(2), grief(1), griefs(1), illness(3), sick(1), sickness(14), sicknesses(1)." Francis Brown, Samuel Rolles Driver, and Charles Augustus Briggs, *Enhanced Brown-Driver-Briggs Hebrew and English Lexicon* (Oak Harbor, WA: Logos Research Systems, 2000), 318. Brown-Driver-Briggs state, "חֳלִי S[2483] TWOT[655a] GK[2716] n.m. Dt 28:59 sickness, חֳלִי Dt 28:61 + 8 times; חֳלִי Dt 7:15 + 2 times; sf. חָלְיוֹ Is 38:9 + 7 times + Ec 5:16 (where del. sf., *cf.* Vrss Now); pl. חֳלָיִם Dt 28:59, 2 חֳלָיִים Ch 21:15, חֳלָיֵנוּ Is 53:4;—*sickness, disease* Dt 7:15; 28:59, 61 1 K 17:17 2 K 1:2; 8:8, 9; 13:14 Is 38:9 2 Ch 16:12⁰; 21:15⁰, 19 ψ 41:4 Ec 6:2; of the suffering servant of ʺ Is 53:3, 4 (in both ‖ מַכְאֹב); of rich man Ec 5:16 (read וָחֳלִי, v. supr.); *incurable disease* 2 רָפֵא לְאֵין מַרְפֵּא ח' Ch 21:18; *recover from sickness* חִיה מֵחָלִי Is 38:9; metaph. of distress of land Ho 5:13 (‖ מָזוֹר), Is 1:5 Je 10:19; = *wound*, of violence in Jerusalem Je 6:7 (‖ מַכָּה)."

mental.[9] Richard L. Mayhue, dean and professor of Theology and Pastoral Ministries at the Master's Seminary, states, "The Hebrew words translated 'griefs' (חֳלִי [*ḥŏlî,* 'sickness, weakness']) and 'sorrows' (מַכְאוֹב [*măḵ·ʾōḇ,* 'mental, emotional pain, anguish']) in Is 53:3, 4, 10 can legitimately refer to either physical infirmities, mental pain, or spiritual problems."[10] Mayhue continues, "The 'scourging' or 'wounds' (53:5) received by Christ, translated חַבּוּרָה (*ḥăb·bû·rāh,* 'stripe, blow'), can speak of actual physical wounds (Gn 4:23; Ex 21:25) or the spiritual afflictions of sin (Ps 38:5; Is 1:6)."[11]

By examining the Hebrew words from which the English words *infirmity, sickness, disease, pain, anguish,* and *sorrow* are translated from in Is 53:4–5, it seems apparent that the suffering servant, the Messiah, carried or took upon him the sickness, disease, pain, and anguish of physical, mental-emotional, and spiritual suffering. Bruce R. Reichenbach, professor of Philosophy at Augsburg College, states, "The fourth servant song (Is 52:13–53:12) is central for developing this motif....One thing immediately striking about this passage is the author's connection of sickness and sin."[12] According to Christopher R. Sietz, an American Old Testament scholar, theologian, and Senior Research Professor of Biblical Interpretation at the Toronto School of Theology, the servant was

9 Brown, Driver and Briggs, *Enhanced Brown-Driver-Briggs Hebrew and English Lexicon*, 456. Brown, Driver and Briggs state, "†מַכְאוֹב S^{4341} TWOT^{940b} GK^{4799} n.m. ψ 32:10 pain;—מ׳ abs. Ec 1:18 + 2 times; cstr. ψ 69:27; sf. מַכְאֹבִי (מַכְאוֹבִי) ψ 38:18 + 3 times, etc.; pl. מַכְאוֹבִים ψ 32:10 Ec 2:23; מַכְאֹבוֹת Is 53:3; sf. מַכְאֹבָיו Ex 3:7; מַכְאֹבֵינוּ Is 53:4;—1. *pain,* physical, Ex 3:7 (|| עֳנִי; *cf.* מִפְּנֵי נֹגְשָׂיו in context); 2 Ch 6:29 (|| נֶגַע); Jb 33:19. 2. of *mental pain,* ψ 32:10 (of troubles of wicked), of Babylon Je 51:8; ψ 38:18; 69:27 (as result of sin; of 'י's servant); in 'י's word to Baruch Je 45:3 (|| יָגוֹן, אֲנָחָה), *cf.* of Israel in distress Je 30:15 (|| שֶׁבֶר), of Jerus. La 1:12$^{()}$, 18, Ec 1:18 (יוֹסִיף דַּעַת יוֹסִיף מַכ׳); 2:23 (|| כַּעַס עִנְיָנוֹ); partic. of suffering servant of י׳ Is 53:3, 4 (both || חֳלִי)."

10 Richard L. Mayhue, "For What Did Christ Atone in Isa 53:4–5," *Master's Seminary Journal* 6, no. 2 (September 1, 1995): 126.

11 Mayhue, "For What Did Christ Atone," 128.

12 Bruce R. Reichenbach, "By His Stripes We Are Healed," *Journal of the Evangelical Theological Society* 41, no. 4 (December 1, 1998): 551.

bearing or carrying something that was not his alone, but for others as well. Sietz states that "since we should not consider the repetition of phrases used of the servant ('sickness' and 'wounds') applied also to the 'we' voices as accidental, a new effect is achieved. The servant is confessed actively to be bearing conditions that belong to the confessors, as they see it. 'Surely he has borne our griefs and carried our sorrows'—that is, his natural and/or afflicted condition was made to serve the purpose of bearing something not naturally his alone, but rightly accruing to others."[13]

Scholars and theologians have differing views as to the precise nature of the atonement accomplished in Is 53:4–5; consequently, there is a risk of misunderstanding the healing motif that the writer of these verses alludes to. Reichenbach elaborates, "Through the centuries Christian theologians have employed diverse motifs—the economics of ransom (Origen, Gregory of Nyssa), judicial proceedings (Anselm), warfare and conquest (Aulen), educational training by example (Socinius, Abelard), and sacrificial rites—to interpret the complexity of atonement. To these Isaiah adds another: healing through the suffering of another." [14] Those who maintain a cessationist position on the *charisms* of the Spirit (including the *charism* of healing) invariably argue that the Is 53:4–5 verses apply only to the issue of atonement for sin.[15] It is important to note that despite the fact that the word *atonement* is not used

---

13 Christopher R. Sietz, "The Book of Isaiah 40–66: Introduction, Commentary, and Reflection," in *The New Interpreter's Bible*, vol. 12 (Nashville, TN: Abingdon Press, 2001), 465–6.

14 Reichenbach, "By His Stripes," 551.

15 Cessationism is principally the belief that the *charismata* of the Holy Spirit ceased after the completion of the canon of scripture and the end of the apostolic age. The cessationist position primarily states that present-day *charisms* of the Holy Spirit (1 Cor 12:7–11) and present-day apostles and prophets (Eph 2:20, 4:11) are no longer in operation. For a thorough examination of cessationism, see Jon Mark Ruthven, *On the Cessation of the Charismata: The Protestant Polemic on Post-Biblical Miracles* (Tulsa, OK: Word & Spirit Press, 2011), *passim*.

in Is 53, the concept of atonement is imbedded within the passage. According to Reichenbach, "the atonement for sin is clearly described by Is 53:5 'But he was pierced for our transgressions, he was crushed for our iniquities.'"[16] In applying atonement to Is 53, W. Kelly Bokovay, an evangelical theologian who writes from a cessationist position, argues that the Day of Atonement in Lv 16 dealt with sin, not sickness.[17] Opponents of physical healing in the Is 53 passage contend that the emphasis relates to salvation from sin, not sickness and disease.[18] But these cessationist arguments simply fail to explain the simple meaning of the language in the passage describing the suffering servant bearing the "sickness" and "mental pain" of God's people in Is 53:4. Others, like Jeffrey Niehus, professor of Old Testament at Gordon-Conwell Theological Seminary, insist that the passage primarily refers to atonement for sin; however, physical healing is available through the cross of Christ as a consequence of sin being atoned for.[19]

However, both Old Testament thought and the nature of Levitical instructions regarding the offering for atonement imply that in ancient Israel a connection was seen between sin and sickness.[20] Kelsey states, "In the Mishnah, and also later in the Talmud, we find the conviction that sin is the root cause of illness."[21] According to Reichenbach, "Not only did serious sins

---

16 Reichenbach, "By His Stripes," 554.

17 W. Kelly Bokovay, "The Relationship of Physical Healing to the Atonement," *Didaskalia* (Otterburne, MB) 3, no. 1 (October 1, 1991): 28; Mayhue, "For What Did Christ Atone," 124.

18 Bokovay, "Relationship," 30; Mayhue, "For What Did Christ Atone," 127. Cf. Ruthven, *Cessation*, footnotes 11–15 on pages 4–6 for an extensive list of books and articles supporting cessationism.

19 Jeffery Niehaus, "Old Testament Foundations: Signs and Wonders in Prophetic Ministry and the Substitutionary Atonement of Isaiah 53," in *The Kingdom and the Power*, ed. Gary S. Grieg and Kevin N. Springer (Ventura, CA: Regal Books, 1993), 49–50.

20 Reichenbach, "By His Stripes," 551–2.

21 Kelsey, *Healing and Christianity*, 31.

and unintentional sins demand atonement, it also was required for certain illnesses that made a person unclean—such as infectious skin diseases or unusual bodily discharges, as when a woman's menstrual period lasted longer than normal—but that were not considered results of sin."[22] Levitical law required atonement for sin and for prolonged illnesses as well, however not for every illness or condition.[23] Hebrew thought and practice connects illness with spirituality, which is likely the reason the writer of Is 53 links atonement for sin and sickness in this passage. Not all sickness was tied to sin; however, the understanding was that some sickness was related to sin. Reichenbach assesses that "The linkage between sin, sickness, suffering and death forms a background motif for Isaiah in the Servant song of chapters 52–53. For him there is no difficulty in moving between the two in prophetic poetic parallelism."[24]

In addition to Hebrew culture, other ancient Middle Eastern cultural norms viewed a connection between sin and sickness. According to Gerhard Kittel, Gerhard Friedrich, and Geoffrey William Bromiley, in their *Theological Dictionary of the New Testament*, which is a standard for many scholars, many Babylonian words relate sin and sickness, Greek mythology connects the avenging of wrongs with pestilence, and Egyptian thought links sickness to punishment for offenses.[25] Hebrew and other ancient cultures saw a link between sickness, disease, sin, and spirituality. The writer of Is 53 was most likely influenced not only by Hebrew thought, but by other cultural understandings of the relationships between sin and sickness.

---

22 Reichenbach, "By His Stripes," 552.

23 Ibid.

24 Ibid., 553.

25 Gerhard Kittel, Gerhard Friedrich, and Geoffrey William Bromiley, eds., *Theological Dictionary of the New Testament, Abridged in One Volume* (Grand Rapids, MI: W. B. Eerdmans, 1985), 655.

Critics of the concept of the servant in Is 53 carrying our sickness and disease occasionally admit that their exegetical analysis of the passage has weaknesses, or that some element of healing is available through the atonement. According to Bokovay, "The word studies are not conclusive; verse 4 could pertain to vicarious or non-vicarious bearing of sin or sickness."[26] Mayhue, in arguing against healing in the atonement, admits that the noun used in Is 53:5, חַבּוּרָה (ḥăb·bû·rā, "stripe, blow"), refers to "wounds from physical abuse."[27] Niehaus also acknowledges that healing is made possible by the atonement: "Because of Christ's atonement, God has sent healings and many other gifts of the Holy Spirit to His Church."[28] Niehaus continues by quoting Gordon Fee, professor emeritus of New Testament Studies at Regent College in Vancouver, who subjectively views healing in the atonement: "As Gordon Fee has observed, 'Healing is provided for [in the atonement] because the atonement brought release from the consequences of sin; nonetheless, since we have not yet received the redemption of our bodies, suffering and death are still our lot until the resurrection.'"[29] The primary problems most of the critics have with the concept of physical healing in the Is 53 passage are a result of 1) a misunderstanding as a whole of Hebrew thought and practice, 2) their exegetical approach to looking at this passage, and 3) their prejudiced bias against the *charisms* of the Spirit and miracles for today.

According to Ruthven, Protestant critics of healing tend to demythologize or allegorize references to healing in both testaments: "Protestants have a strong bias to 'demythologize' or allegorize references to healing, in both testaments: since to them

---

26 Bokovay, "Relationship," 31.

27 Mayhue, "For What Did Christ Atone," 137.

28 Niehaus, "Old Testament Foundations," 50.

29 Gordon D. Fee, *The Disease of the Health and Wealth Gospels* (Costa Mesa, CA: The Word for Today, 1979), 19, quoted in Niehaus, "Old Testament Foundations," 50.

miracles of healing are irrelevant today, they can only be used to talk about the 'real' salvation, that is, from sin. Interestingly, in the Synoptics, the *soter*-family of words always refers to healing as the obvious referent."[30]

Arguments by David Hume, an eighteenth-century Scottish philosopher, historian, economist, and essayist known especially for his philosophical empiricism and skepticism, during the Enlightenment have only further exacerbated the unbelief and cessationist position of many in the church with regard to supernatural ministry. Ruthven states, "The Enlightenment era is generally regarded as the watershed in thought about miracles."[31] Ruthven further states, "Here the cessationist polemic was pushed past its ultimate limit, when the Deists challenged not only the possibility of post-biblical miracles but even the possibility of their ever having occurred at all."[32] Keener summarizes Hume's antimiracle theory accurately in this statement: "Hume works in a deductive circle, as scholars often note. He argues, based on 'experience,' that miracles do not happen, yet dismisses credible eyewitness testimony for miracles (i.e., *others'* experience) on his assumption that miracles do not happen."[33] Keener continues regarding Hume's assumptions against miracles, "It is academically illegitimate to marginalize voices that affirm miracles simply by citing a nonexistent philosophic consensus against miracles."[34]

---

30 Jon Mark Ruthven, e-mail message to author, February 22, 2012.

31 Ruthven, *Cessation*, 24.

32 Ibid., 25.

33 Keener, *Miracles*, 1:108. Keener provides strong theological basis for miracles and healing today; additionally, he documents in detail healing accounts on a global scale.

34 Ibid.

The primary issue many scholars, theologians, and ministers have with bodily healing in the atoning work of the suffering servant of Is 53 (i.e., Jesus Christ) is due to a theological bias that presupposes miracles, healings, and other *charisms* of the Spirit are not for today.

Chapter 4

MATTHEW'S LINK TO ISAIAH

MATTHEW 8:16–17

" That evening they brought to him many who were possessed with demons; and he cast out the spirits with a
word, and cured all who were sick. This was to fulfill what had
been spoken through the prophet Isaiah, 'He took our infirmities
and bore our diseases'" (Mt 8:16–17 NRSV). Perhaps the clearest
New Testament identification of Christ with the suffering servant
of Is 53 is the Mt 8:16–17 passage. As previously mentioned, both
the New Testament and early church tradition link the suffering
servant in Is 53 to Jesus Christ and his sacrificial death. Bokovay,
although a critic of healing in the atonement, links the Matthean
Jesus to the atoning servant of Is 53: "Matthew is not only tying
Jesus to the Servant here, but he is also showing that Jesus' healing ministry is evidence of His Messiahship and a foreshadowing
or preview of Jesus as the One to deal with the ultimate illness of

sin through the cross."[1] However, Reichenbach links Matthew's understanding of "Jesus' healing of the sick who come to him in droves as fulfilling the Servant passage (Mt 8:16, 17). Jesus comes as the promised healer of his people, one who can heal by forgiving sins (9:1–8). For Matthew, Jesus carries out the dual healing ministry prophesied by Isaiah."[2] It becomes apparent that the Matthean Jesus is not only a healer, but one who is linked to the suffering servant of Is 53.

In Mt 8:17, the Greek word for *bore* is *bastázō*. The primary meanings of the word are to "to lift up," "to bear away," and "to pilfer."[3] Often the meaning is "to bear" (Jn 16:12; Rom 15:1; Gal 5:10; 6:2, 5).[4] Paul's use of the word *bastázō* in Gal 6:2, 5 translates to "bear" and to "carry" in English (NRSV); the idea in these verses is to bear burdens of others and to carry one's own load. In either case, the implied meaning is to carry something of weight. Matthew's use of *bastázō* in Mt 8:17 implies a forward view of the cross when Jesus would carry the sins and diseases of humanity. The Greek word for disease in this verse is *nósos*, meaning primarily "sickness."[5]

At the turn of the twentieth century, resurgence in the healing ministry in the body of Christ began to emerge. One of the forerunners was Adoniram Judson (A. J.) Gordon, a nineteenth-century

---

1 Bokovay, "Relationship," 32.

2 Reichenbach, "By His Stripes," 555.

3 Gerhard Kittel, Geoffrey W. Bromiley, and Gerhard Friedrich, eds., *Theological Dictionary of the New Testament*, vol. 1 (Grand Rapids, MI: W. B. Eerdmans, 1964), 596. Kittel, Bromiley, and Friedrich state, "Found in the NT 27 times, 8 in Luke, often par. with αἴρω or φέρω. Relatively rare in the LXX, the equivalent of נשׂא as βάσταγμα is of משׂא. Corresponding Heb. terms acc. to Schlatter are סבל and טען. The basic meaning is uncertain. In the NT it means a. 'to lift up' (Jn. 10:31), b. 'to bear away' (Jn. 20:15), 'to pilfer' (Jn. 12:6; cf. Jos. Ant., 1, 316: Laban to Jacob: ἱερά τε πάτρια βαστάσας οἴχη)."

4 Kittel, Friedrich, and Bromiley, "Theological Dictionary," 1:596.

5 Kittel, Friedrich, and Bromiley, "Theological Dictionary–Abridged," 655. Kittel, Friedrich, and Bromiley state, "*nósos*, of uncertain etymology, means 'sickness,' 'plague,' 'epidemic'; also 'calamity,' 'licentiousness.'"

Baptist pastor and founder of Gordon College and Gordon-Conwell Theological Seminary, who believed that healing was found in the atonement and available through faith in Christ. His book, *The Ministry of Healing*, was influential in the early Pentecostal healing movement. Gordon linked bodily healing with the atoning work of Christ and viewed Mt 8:16–17 as "a deep and suggestive truth that we have Christ set before us as the sickness-bearer as well as the sin-bearer of His people."[6] Gordon continues this thought: "Something more than sympathetic fellowship with our sufferings is evidently referred to here. The yoke of His cross by which He lifted our iniquities took hold also of our diseases; so that it is in some sense true that as God 'made him to be sin for us, who knew no sin' (2 Cor 5:21), so He made Him to be sick for us, who knew no sickness."[7] Gordon succinctly explains what Christ did for us on the cross, in the atonement: "In other words the passage seems to teach that Christ endured vicariously our diseases as well as our iniquities."[8]

Ruthven, commenting on Benjamin Breckinridge (B. B.) Warfield, a professor of theology at Princeton Seminary from 1887 to 1921, and his cessationist argument in *Counterfeit Miracles* against faith healers (which included Gordon), states, "Mt 8:17 served faith healers to show that healing was in some way guaranteed in the atonement of Christ, who bore on the cross not only sins but sicknesses as well."[9] Spence-Jones explains that "Natural healing, as we see in the New Testament, and especially in the miracles of Christ, is a symbol of spiritual healing, and also a pledge of it. In the gospels, 'to be saved,' and 'to be made whole,' are represented by the

---

6 A. J. Gordon, "The Ministry of Healing," in *Healing: The Three Great Classics on Divine Healing*, ed. Jonathan L. Graf (Camp Hill, PA: Christian Publications, Inc., 1992), 130.

7 Ibid.

8 Ibid.

9 Ruthven, *Cessation*, 90.

same Greek word."[10] Mayhue argues that the Matthean reference to Is 53:4 and Christ "bearing" or "carrying" our sicknesses means that he is "taking away" their sicknesses, but not in a substitutionary sense; it was illustrative.[11] Bokovay argues that what Christ did in Capernaum cannot be linked to his atoning work on the cross; it is an illustrative use of Is 53:4.[12]

Despite the exegetical efforts of Mayhue, Bokovay, and others, this is an error with the intent and definition of the Greek words used in this passage. They fail to recognize the relevance the writer of Matthew sees when he recalls the events that took place in the ministry of Christ and his atoning work on the cross. Matthew was clearly connecting the two, not only to confirm the divinity of Christ, but to illustrate the power of the cross and the kingdom of God to his readers. Kittel, Friedrich, and Bromiley state, "The NT refers Is 53 to Jesus, although more in terms of violent death than sickness. Mt 8:17 specifically quotes Is 53:4 in relation to the fact that in bearing away illnesses Jesus also bears them, i.e., takes the needs of the sick to himself (cf. 15:30ff.)."[13] They continue this thought: "The early church does not depict a sick Christ. It refers Is 53:4 to the crucifixion and sees in the healing and teaching Christ the mighty Helper. A sign of increasing Hellenization is the growing tendency to take the infirmities and diseases of Mt 8:17 figuratively."[14]

---

10 Spence-Jones, *Exodus*, 23–24. Spence-Jones continues, "We may state the relation thus: (1) Natural healing is the symbol of spiritual healing. (2) Spiritual healing, in turn, is a pledge of the ultimate removal of all natural evils (Rv 21:4). (3) Each separate experience of healing is a pledge of the whole. It is a fresh testimony to the truth that God is a healer (cf. Ps 103:1–4). Every recovery from sickness is thus, in a way, the preaching of a gospel. It pledges a complete and perfect healing—entire deliverance from natural and spiritual evils—if only we will believe, obey, and use God's method."

11 Mayhue, "For What Did Christ Atone,"133.

12 Bokovay, "Relationship," 32.

13 Kittel, Friedrich, and Bromiley, "Theological Dictionary–Abridged," 656.

14 Ibid., 657.

Chapter 5

THE COMMISSIONING ACCOUNTS

In Mt 10:1, Mk 3:14–15, and Lk 9:1–2, Jesus "summoned his twelve disciples and gave them authority over unclean spirits, to cast them out, and to cure every disease and every sickness" (Mt 10:1 NRSV). He continues, "As you go, proclaim the good news, 'The kingdom of heaven has come near.' Cure the sick, raise the dead, cleanse the lepers, cast out demons. You received without payment; give without payment" (Mt 10:7–8 NRSV). Mark's gospel continues the commissioning theme of the twelve: "So they went out and proclaimed that all should repent. They cast out many demons, and anointed with oil many who were sick and cured them" (Mk 6:12–13 NRSV).

They were given authority, ἐξουσία (*exousía*, the right or power),[1] over sickness, disease, and unclean spirits. They were instructed to exercise the authority they were given by God to cure, *therapeúō* (heal),[2] the afflicted, not to merely pray for them. They were called to be an extension of the very ministry that Jesus demonstrated. This ministry was not limited to the twelve, but Jesus commissioned the seventy in Lk 10:9 to enter the cities and "cure the sick who are there, and say to them, 'The kingdom of God has come near to you'" (NRSV). Later, in verse 17, the seventy return with joy, exclaiming, "Lord, in your name even the demons submit to us!" (NRSV). Kelsey writes of these commissioning passages, "If one writes this off as mythology and says that Jesus and his followers were *only* interested in the life to come (eschatology), one does real violence to the text."[3]

---

1 Kittel, Friedrich, and Bromiley, "Theological Dictionary–Abridged," 238. Kittel, Friedrich, and Bromiley state, "*exousía* 1. This word denotes first the 'ability' to perform an action. 2. It then means the 'right,' 'authority,' 'permission' conferred by a higher court: a. the possibility granted by government; b. the right in various social relationships, e.g., that of parents, masters, or owners. The LXX uses the term for right, authority, etc. in the legal sense and also as it is given by God, e.g., in the law. Formally, NT usage is closest to that of the LXX. *exousía* is God's power, the power given to Jesus, or the power given by Jesus to his disciples." Cf. Johannes P. Louw and Eugene Albert Nida, *Greek-English Lexicon of the New Testament: Based on Semantic Domains*, 2nd ed (New York: United Bible Societies, 1996), 2:92, "ἐξουσία a authority to rule: 37.35 b jurisdiction: 37.36 c symbol of authority: 37.37 d ruler: 37.38 e control: 37.13 f power: 76.12 g supernatural power: 12.44 h right to judge: 30.122 ἐξουσία: unit ἄρχων τῆς ἐξουσίας τοῦ ἀέρος supernatural power 12.44."

2 Ibid., 331–32. Kittel, Friedrich, and Bromiley state, "*Therapeúō* 1. This word, in secular Greek, means a. 'to serve,' 'to be serviceable,' and b. 'to care for the sick,' 'to treat,' 'to cure' (also figuratively). 2. The same senses may be found in Judaism (cf. 'to serve' in Esth. 1:1b and 'to heal' in Sir. 18:19). Philo refers to healing of both body and soul. 3. In view of the miracles of Jesus, one might expect many parallels among the rabbis of his day, but in fact we have only isolated instances. 4.a. In the NT *therapeúō* never means 'to serve' in a secular sense, and only once in Acts 17:25 does it denote worship. Paul's point here is that the true God has no cultic dwelling and does not need a cultic ministry, so that the *therapeúein* that is suitable for idols is inappropriate to him. b. A much more common use is for 'healing,' not merely in the sense of medical treatment, but in the sense of the real healing that the Messiah brings."

3 Kelsey, *Healing and Christianity*, 81.

The gospel of the kingdom of God is a demonstration of the reality that the kingdom of heaven is at hand because of the signs, wonders, and healings that occur. It is more than verbal proclamation; it is backed by God's power to heal and restore. According to Ruthven, "The *Kingdom of God* in the NT is described directly or indirectly as God's *ruling power in action.*"[4] Ruthven also states, "When Jesus is 'teaching' about the kingdom of God, he is 'training' people for entrance into the realm of God's healing, exorcising and saving power."[5] Jesus brought the people into contact with the rule of God's kingdom, and in so doing, gave the disciples authority and opportunity to walk in this same realm and to heal and impart this to others as they had received: "You received without payment; give without payment" (Mt 10:8 NRSV).

The ministries of the twelve and of the seventy were extensions of the mission and authority of Jesus. They were trained in how to bring about God's kingdom and rule on earth, and were forerunners of a discipleship movement based on the authority and miraculous power that Jesus intended to continue until the *parousia*, his second coming. Pheme Perkins, professor of New Testament Theology at Boston College, comments on Christ sending out the twelve in Mark's gospel, stating, "He now sends them out with the authority to expel demons (vv. 7, 12–13) as well as to preach the news of the kingdom...the Twelve participate directly in Jesus' own activity of bringing about the rule of God...he intends for them to preach and exorcise (3:14*b*–15; 6:7, 12)."[6] Perkins continues, "Since

---

4 Jon Mark Ruthven, *What's Wrong with Protestant Theology?* (Unpublished manuscript, 2011), 138. For finished manuscript, see Jon Mark Ruthven *What's Wrong with Protestant Theology?* (Tulsa, OK: Word & Spirit Press, 2012).

5 Jon Mark Ruthven, DMin Phase 2 cohort notes and lecture, January 23–27, 2012, 16.

6 Pheme Perkins, "The Gospel of Mark: Introduction, Commentary, and Reflections," in *The New Interpreter's Bible*, vol. 8 (Nashville, TN: Abingdon Press, 1996), 594.

their mission is successful, this section demonstrates that the disciples were able to carry out the ministry for which Jesus had chosen them. At the same time, they do not possess independent authority. They are extensions of Jesus' own activity."[7]

Looking at the commissioning account at the end of Matthew's gospel, we see a link between the earlier commissioning accounts and the Great Commission: "And Jesus came and said to them, 'All authority in heaven and on earth has been given to me. Go therefore and make disciples of all the nations, baptizing them in the name of the Father and of the Son and of the Holy Spirit, and teaching them to obey everything that I have commanded you. And remember, I am with you always, to the end of the age'" (Mt 28:18–20 NRSV). Once again, authority is translated from *exousía* (the right or power). The Matthean Jesus is telling the reader, "I have been given the right, authority, and power in heaven and on earth, and I'm sending you in my name and authority." The implication is that he is extending his authority and power to the disciples to make other disciples until he returns. What are they to do? They are to teach others everything that they have been taught. What were they taught? They were primarily taught how to proclaim the good news of the kingdom of God through healing the sick and casting out demons.

In the culture of that day, a disciple was an exact copy of his teacher, so new disciples would be immersed in the life and power

---

7 Perkins, "Gospel of Mark," 8:594.

of the Spirit as were the original disciples.[8] This follows the didactic teaching patterns of rabbis of that time, in which disciples were expected to copy the rabbi's deeds as well as his words.[9] Commenting on the Gospel of Matthew, Senior echoes the same theme, stating that the original disciples were to make new disciples in the same form and "manner affirmed throughout the gospel of Matthew," including the tasks of "proclamation and healing."[10] Perkins, in commenting on the Markan gospel, advocates the continuance of the ministry of Jesus by the early disciples that includes healing of the sick, as the twelve share both the authority of Jesus and his mission.[11] Furthermore, Perkins concludes that those in ministry today are called to a ministry that continues the work of Christ and his mission: "These simple instructions, which reflect the practice of early Christian missionaries, call those engaged in ministry back to the fundamental basis of all preaching, healing, and teaching: the ministry and person of Jesus."[12]

The disciples were taught by Christ in word and demonstration to heal the sick, cast out demons, and proclaim the message of the kingdom of God. There is no evidence that the commissioning accounts and patterns in other portions of the Gospels were not

---

8 Ruthven, DMin Phase 2 cohort notes, 18. Ruthven states, "1) 'authority' here is the same as before: over demons and sickness. 2) Therefore make disciples (=apostles, just as Jesus did), immersing them in the life, power and character of God as expressed in Father, Son and Spirit. A 'disciple' is an exact copy of the teacher (in that culture), so they have 'authority' to deliver and heal. 3) Specifically, what do these disciples learn? 'ALL I have commanded you.' See commissioning accounts, *e.g.*, Lk 9 and 10: 'heal the sick, raise the dead, cast out demons,' etc. 4) Jesus is present always with his total authority (vs 18). He goes everywhere disciples go, empowering them—'to the end of the age/world' (time and place). It is in Jesus' presence with us and with his authority that we go."

9 Ruthven, *What's Wrong*, 178.

10 Donald Senior, *The Gospel of Matthew, Interpreting Biblical Texts* (Nashville, TN: Abingdon Press, 1997), 175–177.

11 Perkins, "Gospel of Mark," 8:596.

12 Ibid.

to be included in the Great Commission account of Mt 28:18–20. Ruthven describes the problem with removing the other commissioning accounts from the Great Commission text of Matthew: "It is claimed that this 'Great Commission' is quite different from the earlier commissioning accounts (Mt 10; Mk 6; Lk 9 and 10) because it merely involves 'teaching' all nations and that there is no mention of miracles in this commission."[13] Ruthven continues, "Given the parallels with the other highly charismatic commissioning accounts, it is clear that the 'Great Commission' means what it says, that is, the same essential charismatic themes of the New Covenant Spirit."[14]

Edgar Krentz, professor emeritus of New Testament at Christ Seminary, views the entire Gospel of Matthew as instruction for Christian discipling, "as a manual for teaching Christian life. This is important to him; he stresses the realization of the gospel in deeds."[15] Krentz concludes that Matthew "gives a new task to the church: to make disciples of the nations around them. His gospel is a resource for the church as it does that, a shaper of life."[16] Quoting Daniel J. Harrington, who was a professor of New Testament at Boston College School of Theology and Ministry, Krentz states: "It is possible to view Mt 28:16–20 as a summary of

---

13 Ruthven, *What's Wrong*, 180–181. Ruthven further identifies the problems as follows: "1) power *exousia* used here is the same as in Lk 9:1; 10:1. 2) The use of the word *therefore*, creates a causal connection with the commission to come: because Jesus has demon casting authority, 'therefore' the disciples are to make other disciples with this kind of authority; 3) they are to be baptized, and to baptize their disciples, not in a ritualized formula, but in the authority and character of the 'name' of the Father, Son and Holy Spirit (the New Covenant Spirit of prophecy and power). 4) They are to make to disciples who replicate the life and mission of their teachers."

14 Ibid., 182.

15 Edgar Krentz, "Missionary Matthew: Matthew 28:16–20 as Summary of the Gospel," *Currents in Theology and Mission* 31, no. 1 (February 1, 2004): 30.

16 Ibid., 31.

the whole Gospel."[17] If the Great Commission account in Mt 28 is a summary of the entire gospel, then one would have to conclude that the commissioning account in Mt 10, with the instructions to heal the sick, perform exorcisms, and even raise the dead, is part of the gospel to be proclaimed and of the discipleship model to be replicated among future disciples. Randy Clark agrees with this assessment of the Great Commission passage in Mt 28:

> This passage indicates that people who become Christians should be taught to do what Jesus taught the disciples to do. Healing the sick and casting out demons top the list, and nothing indicates that those were only meant to be done until the Bible was canonized. As long as we baptize in the name of the Father, the Son and the Holy Spirit, we are to continue teaching the newly baptized to heal the sick and cast out demons.[18]

In Mk 16, we find a similar commissioning account to Mt 28:

> And he said to them, "Go into all the world and proclaim the good news to the whole creation. The one who believes and is baptized will be saved; but the one who does not believe will be condemned. And these signs will accompany those who believe: by using my name they will cast out demons; they will speak in new tongues; they will pick up snakes in their hands, and if they drink any deadly thing, it will not hurt them; they will lay their hands on the sick, and they will recover." (Mk 16:15–18 NRSV)

17 Daniel J. Harrington, *The Gospel of Matthew*, Sacra Pagina 1 (Collegeville, MN: The Liturgical Press, 1991), 415–6, quoted in Krentz, "Missionary Matthew," 31.

18 Bill Johnson and Randy Clark, *The Essential Guide to Healing: Equipping All Christians to Pray for the Sick* (Bloomington, MN: Chosen Books, 2011), 60. Clark and Global Awakening Ministries are mentioned in Brown, *Healing*, Ch. 17 and Keener, *Miracles*, 1:489–91. Clark and Global Awakening associates witness as normative miracles and healings in meetings on an international scale, including in the United States.

While scholars have debated the inclusion of verses 9–20 in the Markan gospel, the tenor of the passage parallels other gospels. This longer ending was "possibly written in the early second century and appended to the Gospel later in the second century. These sentences borrow some motifs from the other Gospels."[19] Many scholars agree with this premise, that while the appropriate ending of the Markan gospel should be 16:8, the tenor of the Gospels would make the longer ending of Mark appropriate.

Robert H. Stein, senior professor of New Testament Interpretation at the Southern Baptist Theological Seminary, states in *The Ending of Mark*, "It is the thesis of this paper that our best-preserved ending of the Gospel of Mark is 16:8. Internal considerations from the Gospel of Mark, however, strongly suggest that this is not the intended ending of the Gospel."[20] Stein goes on to say the ending at verse 8 is incomplete and that "Mark was unable to write his intended ending (perhaps because of martyrdom or persecution or some other reason), however, [this is] only conjecture."[21]

Morna D. Hooker, a British theologian and New Testament scholar, comments, "The gospel of Mark ends abruptly, at 16:8, and early attempts to add an ending show that it was felt to be incomplete. It is possible that the book was never finished or that it was damaged at an early stage."[22] Perkins confirms that the longer

---

19 Coogan, *New Oxford Annotated Bible*, 1824–5; cf. Mk 16.9–20n.

20 Robert H. Stein, "The Ending of Mark," *Bulletin For Biblical Research* 18, no. 1 (January 1, 2008):97.

21 Ibid.

22 Morna D. Hooker, "Mark, The Gospel According to," in *The Oxford Companion to the Bible,* ed. Bruce M. Metzger and Michael D. Coogan (New York: Oxford University Press, 1993), 496.

ending of Mk (16:9–20) was already known by the second century, containing elements of the apostolic tradition found in Acts.[23]

Werner Kelber, professor emeritus in Biblical Studies at Rice University, states, "The ending of the Gospel of Mark is not a conclusion but rather an invitation to consider the implications of Jesus' resurrection for their own involvement in God's kingdom by reconsidering Jesus' Galilean ministry."[24] Raymond Pickett, professor of New Testament at the Lutheran School of Theology at Chicago, writes concerning Kelber's view of this passage, "Kelber, who emphasizes 'Mark's oral legacy,' observes that, 'Jesus' entire life and death constitutes a pedagogical paradigm, inspiring the disciples to learn by imitation and participation.'"[25]

Lindsey P. Pherigo, professor emeritus of New Testament and Early Church History at Saint Paul School of Theology, maintains that through technical study and an understanding consistent with the rest of Mark, "there is good reason for thinking that its principal 'other source' was the original ending itself. It may therefore be regarded as a revised version of the original. The best explanation of why the original ending itself was not

---

23 Perkins, "Gospel of Mark," 8:728–729. Perkins notes in a footnote, "Although not part of the original Gospel of Mark, this ending was declared canonical by the Council of Trent and is the Gospel reading for the feast of St. Mark in the Roman Catholic lectionary."

24 Werner Kelber, *The Oral and the Written Gospel* (Philadelphia: Fortress, 1983), 70, quoted in Raymond Pickett, "Following Jesus in Galilee: Resurrection as Empowerment in the Gospel of Mark," *Currents in Theology and Mission* 32, no. 6 (December 1, 2005): 435.

25 Ibid.

restored is simply that it was now lost except in the memory of oral tradition."[26]

Indeed, the mission of Jesus is replicated in the longer ending of Mark and is consistent with the tenor of the gospel commissioning accounts. The intent of Jesus, as is the case in all of the commissioning accounts, is to train disciples by imitation and participation. His desire is that those who believe in every age would continue his ministry and in turn would train others in the same model of ministry. Irrespective of the best-preserved ending of Mark, the thought, tenor, and intent of Mk 16:9–20 coincide with the discipleship practice of Jesus and his followers.

Proclaiming the kingdom through healings and exorcisms is to be normative for the believer in Christ. According to Gary S. Greig, "The 'signs' that the Lord worked to confirm the preaching of His word included the *gift* of 'speak[ing] in new tongues' (16:17), *deliverance* ('they will drive out demons,' 16:17), and *healing* ('they will place their hands on sick people, and they will get well' 16:18)."[27] A. J. Gordon states, "'These signs shall follow them that believe,' in every generation and period of the Church's history— so the language compels us to conclude...there is no ground for limiting this promise to apostolic times and apostolic men...in any

26 Lindsey P. Pherigo, "The Gospel According to Mark," in *The Interpreter's One-Volume Commentary on the Bible: Introduction and Commentary for Each Book of the Bible Including the Apocrypha*, ed. Charles M. Laymon (Nashville, TN: Abingdon Press, 1971), 671. Pherigo states, "The 'longer ending' appears in almost all of the later manuscripts and therefore in the KJV, as well as most other versions; in the RSV it is placed in a footnote. Technical study makes clear that it comes from a different author and is based on Luke, John, and some other sources. Since it reports, in typical Markan fashion, the disbelief of the disciples and has the risen Jesus upbraiding them severely for their unbelief and hardness of heart (vs. 14), and since it has a typically Markan understanding of the gospel (vss. 15–16)."

27 Gary S. Greig, "The Purpose of Signs and Wonders in the New Testament," in *The Kingdom and the Power,* ed. Gary S. Greig and Kevin N. Springer (Ventura, CA: Regal Books, 1993), 139.

and every age of the Christian dispensation."[28] In Mk 16:20, the statement that the signs follow the preaching of the word, not the apostles, is indicative again that the disciples in every age are to continue the message and mission of Christ in power.

In Jn 14:12 (NRSV) Jesus says, "Very truly, I tell you, the one who believes in me will also do the works that I do and, in fact, will do greater works than these, because I am going to the Father." Similar to Mk 16:17, Jesus gives a promise to believers that they would perform the same types of works that he did. While many would tend to spiritualize the miraculous aspects of his intention in this verse, the potential for believers to continue and operate in the mission of Christ remains. Ruthven elaborates by saying, "Recent scholarship is more nuanced, concluding generally that the evangelist's intention was that 'greater' miracles were to continue among the disciples in that they were to be performed in a more eschatologically advanced era than during the earthly mission of Christ, namely that of the exalted Lord Jesus."[29] According to Clark, "Many New Testament scholars have pointed out that the Greek term *erga* used in John 14:12 to mean 'works' denotes *miraculous works*. So Jesus is saying that anyone who has faith in Him will do the *same miraculous works that He did*."[30] Kelsey says of this passage in John, "It is hard to see how followers who really accepted

---

28 Gordon, 133.

29 Ruthven, *Cessation*, 92–93.

30 Johnson and Clark, *Essential Guide*, 79. Cf. Gary Greig, e-mail message to author, June 24, 2013, [sic] "The Greek term, *erga* 'works,'; when referring to Jesus and God the Father in the Gospel of John, denote miraculous works and are closely related to the .i.*semeia*, 'signs,'; of Jesus. So, for example, the healing of the man born blind in is referred to as '*the works of God (ta erga tou Theou)*' in .i.Jn. 9:3; and as one of '*such signs (toiauta semeia)*' in .i.Jn 9:16. 'The deeds of God and Jesus, specifically miracles;' W. Bauer, F. W. Danker, W. F. Arndt, and F. W. Gingrich, *A Greek-English Lexicon of the New Testament and Other Early Christian Literature* (Chicago: The University of Chicago, 2000) 390, right column; R. C. Trench, *Notes on the Miracles of Our Lord* (London Macmillan, 1856), 6; Rengstorf, '*semeion*,' in G. Kittel, ed., *Theological Dictionary of the New Testament*, vol. 7, 247–248."

such a commission could come back later and ask whether it was God's will or not that sick people be healed sacramentally."[31]

Paul taught and experienced the kingdom from a perspective of power, starting with his own conversion: "For the kingdom of God depends not on talk but on power" (1 Cor 4:20 NRSV). Ruthven states it is "miracle power" that Paul is referring to.[32] Earlier in the First Epistle to the Corinthians, Paul explains a similar theme: "My speech and my proclamation were not with plausible words of wisdom, but with a demonstration of the Spirit and of power, so that your faith might rest not on human wisdom but on the power of God" (1 Cor 2:4–5 NRSV). Paul alludes to a faith that is anchored in the charismatic expression of God in power; human wisdom and reason simply cannot substitute for God's presence and power in teaching and making disciples of the nations. Commenting on 1 Cor 2:4–5 Greig states, "The use of 'Spirit and power' in this passage shows that the 'demonstration' referred not only to conveying spiritual gifts (explicitly referred to in 1 Cor 1:6–7), but also to the signs, wonders, and miracles characteristic of Paul's ministry in Corinth (2 Cor 12:12 *en pase hupomone* 'with great perseverance') and of his ministry in general (Rom 15:18–19)."[33] Greig summarizes this section by stating, "Thus Paul teaches that both the object of one's faith—Christ, the message of the Truth—and God demonstrating the truth by His power in our lives strengthen and reinforce our faith."[34]

Ruthven identifies power with the nature of the kingdom of God: "The *nature* of the Kingdom is expressed in the typical way God reveals himself: in divine power (1 Cor 2:4–5; 4:19–20). Accordingly, true Christian 'preaching' (presenting the Kingdom)

---

31 Kelsey, *Healing and Christianity*, 81.

32 Ruthven, *What's Wrong*, 138.

33 Greig, "The Purpose of Signs," 149.

34 Ibid.

is necessarily expressed in *dunamis* (miracle power Rom 15:19; 2 Cor 12:12; 1 Thes 1:5; 1 Pt 4:6)."[35] Clark explains the importance of 1 Cor 2:2–5 in terms of preaching with a demonstration of power: "This famous passage indicates the importance of preaching with a demonstration of the Spirit's power. The new believers at Corinth were the actual evidence of the Spirit's power. But Paul's modus operandi was to communicate the message of the cross, which included Jesus' resurrection and His pouring out of the Holy Spirit as a sign that the Kingdom of God had begun, a Kingdom that was already present, though not yet complete."[36]

35 Ruthven, *What's Wrong*, 139.
36 Johnson and Clark, *Essential Guide*, 77.

Chapter 6

Are Any among You Sick?

JAMES 5:14–16

One of the earliest practices of caring for the sick was derived from Jas 5:14–16: "Are any among you sick? They should call for the elders of the church and have them pray over them, anointing them with oil in the name of the Lord. The prayer of faith will save the sick, and the Lord will raise them up; and anyone who has committed sins will be forgiven" (NRSV). The writer of James instructs those who are sick to request the elders of the church to pray for them and anoint them with oil; the writer's intent is to inform the readers that healing is made available through the act of anointing with oil and faith-filled prayer through Christ. In this passage, a model of healing is described that was frequently used by the early church, providing a framework for healing in the church, both past and present.

The writer of James mentions the audience as the "twelve tribes in the Dispersion" (Jas 1:1, NRSV). Martin C. Albl, professor of

Religious Studies at Presentation College, states, "Scholarship has come to no firm conclusions regarding either authorship or audience."[1] While the exact author or audience is unclear in James, the letter provides historical access to the basic beliefs of healing in the Christian community of that time.[2] The passage establishes a physical, as well as spiritual and emotional, healing motif in the early church. Albl states, "While ἀσθενέω (astheneō) can in fact refer metaphorically to any type of weakness (e.g., Rom 14:1; 1 Cor 8:7–12), a consensus of commentators rightly understands this term to refer specifically to bodily ailments."[3] In Jas 5:13, the writer distinguishes between "suffering: κακοπαθέω" and "sickness/weakness: ἀσθενέω" in verse 14. As Albl points out, "Κακοπαθέω is a more general term for any type of suffering; its pairing with εὐθυμέω ('cheerful') in this verse suggests nonbodily suffering."[4] Albl continues, "While one must take care not to impose modern conceptions of 'physical' (as opposed to 'mental' or 'spiritual') reality on ancient texts, the primary reference in this passage is clearly to ailments of the body."[5] This passage establishes a precedent for physical healing, both at the time of its writing and presently through Christ, as it gives no indication of a cessation of such ministry. The early church saw bodily healing as a primary motif of this passage in James; however, mental, emotional, and spiritual healing is also made available through Christ

---

1 Martin C. Albl, "'Are Any among You Sick?' The Health Care System in the Letter of James," *Journal of Biblical Literature* 121, no. 1 (March 1, 2002): 124. Albl continues in the footnote, "A scholarly consensus holds that James purports to be written by James, the brother of Jesus, leader of the Jerusalem church until his death around the year 62. Yet, whether James is penned directly by him, represents a collection of his teaching revised by a later editor, or is simply a pseudonymous work is unclear. Proposals have located the audience from Palestine to Hellenistic Egypt to Rome."

2 Ibid., 125.

3 Ibid.

4 Ibid.

5 Ibid.

and is intrinsic to this passage and should not be overlooked, as Warrington demonstrates.[6]

Keith Warrington, director of Doctoral Studies at Regents Theological College, writes, "The term 'sick' (5:14) is a translation of *asthenéō*. The latter is used in Jewish, Christian and secular Greek writings of that era to refer to a variety of conditions including spiritual weakness, physical weakness and sickness as well as less common meanings that relate to other forms of weakness."[7] Warrington proposes that while *asthenéō* refers to physical illness, one cannot rule out other forms of weakness intended by God to be healed in this passage: discouragement, spiritual weakness, emotional weariness, and fear, for example.[8] The writer of Luke describes in chapter four that Jesus read and quoted from Is 61:1, 2. A task of the Messiah was to "bind up the brokenhearted," or simply put to "heal those who are broken or wounded." To limit this healing to the brokenness of man's spiritual nature before Christ would be a mistake, just as it would be a mistake to limit God's healing virtue to only physical ailments. Christ died for the entire healing and salvation of man's being—spirit, soul, and body. The obvious intention by the writer of James is to ensure the church understood that healing through prayer and anointing of oil was complete—spiritually, physically, and mentally.

Mk 6:13 states, "They cast out many demons, and anointed with oil many who were sick and cured them" (NRSV). Concerning this text, Pheme Perkins comments, "The early Christian practice of anointing the sick (cf. Jas 5:14) is attached to the mission of the disciples (v. 13). This correspondence encourages readers to see the origins of early Christian missionary activity in the authority and

---

6 Keith Warrington, "James 5:14–18: Healing Then and Now," *International Review of Mission* 93, no. 370–371 (July 1, 2004): 347–51.

7 Ibid., 347.

8 Ibid., 347–8.

ministry of Jesus."[9] According to Dionisio Borobio, professor of Liturgy and Sacraments at the Pontifical University of Salamanca, "Mark clearly establishes a direct connection between the rite of anointing with oil and healing the sick, within a broader religious and evangelizing context, which supposes a call to conversion and liberation from all evil and the power of the devil."[10] Amanda Porterfield, professor of Religion at Florida State University, writes that an early second-century bishop "identified care of the sick as one of the chief tasks for which church elders were responsible. A guidebook for Christian communities written in Rome around 215 instructed bishops to pay house calls on sick members. In their ministrations to the sick, Christians adopted a simple rite, based on descriptions of healings Jesus performed, of anointing the sick with oil 'in the name of the Lord.'"[11] The church and Mediterranean culture viewed the anointing of oil as more than symbolic and medicinal, especially in Hellenistic and Jewish contexts.[12] According to Albl,

> Anointing (ἀλείφω) with olive oil (ἔλαιον) was a charged symbol in this cultural area. Oil was used medicinally, but was also employed in specifically cultic contexts to mark objects or people as sacred. In general, its use marks an individual's transition from an "ordinary" reality to a special or even sacred state. In ancient Jewish context, ritual anointing marks a person or object as specifically chosen by God (the ritual is usually associated with a king, but priests, prophets, and even cultic objects were also anointed), here

9 Perkins, "Gospel of Mark," 8:594–5.

10 Dionisio Borobio, "An Enquiry into Healing Anointing in the Early Church," in *Pastoral Care of the Sick* (London: SCM, 1991), 40.

11 Amanda Porterfield, *Healing in the History of Christianity* (New York: Oxford University Press, 2005), 47.

12 Albl, "Are Any among You Sick?,"137.

too one sees a movement from ordinary to sacred status. More generally, oil symbolized well-being and health.[13]

Ruthven contends that anointing with oil and prayer for the sick was a common practice in the early church. In countering Warfield's cessationist view of miracles and his polemic that the anointing oil had medicinal value only, Ruthven argues that the practice of anointing the sick with oil came from the "earliest strata of Christian charismatic tradition, i.e., Mk 6:13, when, after the disciples were given spiritual power (ἐξουσία) over evil spirits... they 'drove out many demons and anointed many sick people with oil and healed them.' Here, clearly, is not a description of medical missionaries, but of those, who like Jesus, were empowered for spiritual battle."[14]

A significant element of Jas 5:15 is the understanding of the Greek word *sōzō*, used in this text, from which *save* is translated in the NRSV. The word has three primary meanings—to deliver, to save, or to heal.[15] The word *sōzō* (σῴζω) is used interchangeably in the New Testament for salvation from sin (Acts 4:12, Rom 10:9, Eph 2:8), for healing (Mt 9:22, Mk 6:56, Mk 10:52), and for deliverance (exorcism) (Lk 8:36, 2 Tm 4:18, Jude 1:5). Many English translations of Jas 5:15 use the word *save* instead of *heal*, but as previously mentioned, *sōzō* implies salvation from sin, bodily healing (as well as emotional healing), and deliverance from demonic oppression. Explaining *sōzō*, Kelsey writes, "Since in the Greek mind

---

13 Albl, "Are Any among You Sick?," 137–8.

14 Ruthven, *Cessation*, 92.

15 Louw and Nida, vol. 1. Louw and Nida define the word as follows: "σῴζω (pf σέσωκα) a rescue: 21.18 b save: 21.27 c heal: 23.136. 21.18 σῴζωᵃ; σωτηρίαᵃ, ας *f*: to rescue from danger and to restore to a former state of safety and well being—'to deliver, to rescue, to make safe, deliverance.' 21.27 σῴζωᵇ: to cause someone to experience divine salvation—'to save.' 23.136 ἰάομαιᵃ; ἴασις, εως *f*; σῴζωᶜ; διασῴζωᵇ: to cause someone to become well again after having been sick—'to heal, to cure, to make well, healing.'"

the saving of the body implied moving one step on the way toward salvation of the entire being, this word was related by implication to the whole idea of salvation. From it the theological word soteriology, or the study of salvation, is derived."[16]

According to Clark, "Jerome translated the word as 'save,' instead. This eventually led to changing the Anointing of the Sick, which was not reserved for the dying, to Last Rights or Extreme Unction, a Roman Catholic set of sacraments usually given to a dying person not expected to recover."[17] Kelsey explains, "The idea of being saved from spiritual death cannot be supported, however, by the original Greek text. The sense of the words in Greek is healed, cured, saved from illness or death."[18] The words *save, heal,* or *deliver* could be used interchangeably in Jas 5:15 and in other New Testament passages using the word *sōzō*; however, in the totality of what God has done for us in Christ, *heal* is perhaps the most accurate English word.

When observing the ministry of Jesus, the gospel accounts often link deliverance (exorcism) with healing: "That evening they brought to him many who were possessed with demons; and he cast out the spirits with a word, and cured all who were sick. This was to fulfill what had been spoken through the prophet Isaiah, 'He took

---

16 Kelsey, *Healing and Christianity*, 87.

17 Johnson and Clark, *Essential Guide*, 96. Cf. Kelsey, *Healing and Christianity*, 151, "Jerome addressed the subject of healing but it was not part of his personal experience."

18 Kelsey, *Healing and Christianity*, 92. Kelsey continues, "For centuries the Roman Catholic church officially interpreted this passage to mean the act of saving a person from spiritual death, and supported the meaning with the translation from the Vulgate. It was upon this understanding that the practice of extreme unction was based. Instead of the Latin words *curo* or *sano*, which commonly meant to heal or cure medically, only the word *salvo*, to save, was used in the Vulgate to translate 'save' or 'heal' or 'cure' in this passage. This was a word that came into Latin only in Christian times and carried the peculiar modern meaning of salvation, rather than the meaning of the ordinary words in common usage that referred to physical or mental healing." Cf. Kelsey footnote, "The Latin word *salvo* was probably first used by Lactantius in the third or fourth century AD."

our infirmities and bore our diseases'" (Mt 8:16–17 NRSV). Greig states, "How else could the one word *sōzō* denote both salvation from sin and healing of illness in the New Testament, unless healing was a symbol of God's power to save sinners?"[19] Ruthven adds, "Almost all of the references to 'salvation' (Greek: *sōtēria*) in the Gospels are immediately about healing or deliverance. In the rest of the NT, the term can be more general, including eternal salvation. In the NT, 'salvation' includes the whole person in the present as well as the future. Traditional theology stresses 'salvation' from sin and hell."[20] While many would place the immanent healing motif in James in a strictly eschatological context, Borobio sees both aspects as one, and not in conflict with each other. Borobio states,

> The fact that these verbs [*sosei, egerei*] also carry an eschatological meaning of salvation (eternal life or salvation, resurrection) is not in conflict with their physical meaning of healing. In the closest line of continuity with Christ's ministry to the sick, they must refer to an integral physical-spiritual, present-eschatological, healing or saving. The effect of "saving and strengthening the sick" is not reductive but extensive, not partial but total. Coherent continuity with Christ's ministry to the sick, the Hebrew people's anthropological and biblical conception, comparison with other texts and places, the relationship between temporal and eschatological health, the very fact that our text implies an "open" interpretation...all justify this conclusion.[21]

Likewise, Albl sees the immediate potential for bodily healing and the eschatological aspect of salvation for the individual as one

---

19 Greig, "The Purpose of Signs," 160.

20 Ruthven, DMin Phase 2 cohort notes, 16.

21 Borobio, "Enquiry into Healing," 40.

entity: "The ritual anointing and community prayers move the patient into the realm of both bodily healing and eschatological salvation. The system does not separate the two."[22] The model of healing that James constitutes in this text seems clear: the act of anointing the sick with oil combined with prayer, faith, and confession has divine healing virtues, both presently in bodily healing and in an eschatological salvation context.

---

22 Albl, "Are Any among You Sick?," 143.

Section 2

HISTORICAL CONSIDERATIONS

Chapter 7

HISTORICAL OVERVIEW OF HEALING IN THE CHURCH

Many have taught that the gifts of healing and deliverance ceased with the death of the original apostles and with the completion of the canon of scripture in the fourth century.[1] History demonstrates that healing and deliverance ministry was an integral part of the culture and growth of the church in the early centuries. Early church fathers not only believed that God was still the healer, but actively practiced healing and deliverance centuries after the Apostolic age ended and the canon of scripture was complete.[2] Despite a diminished influence of this ministry during the Middle Ages, Reformation, and Enlightenment era, there has been a renewed emphasis

---

1 Cf. Ruthven, *Cessation* for a complete study of the tenants of cessationism.

2 For texts on healing in the early church see Ramsey MacMullen, *Christianizing the Roman Empire (AD 100–400)* (New Haven, CT: Yale University, 1984); Kelsey, *Healing and Christianity*; Porterfield, *Healing*; Keener, *Miracles*.

upon healing and deliverance ministry since the nineteenth century. According to Craig S. Keener, "By the late nineteenth century, a much broader and more consistent healing movement than among earlier US Protestants grew from the circles that were heavily emphasizing holiness."[3] From about the fifth century through the Enlightenment period, the attitude of the church turned more negative toward healing and deliverance ministry.[4] Yet despite these theological changes in the church related to healing and deliverance ministry, these graces have continued throughout church history and into our postmodern era.[5]

In order to gain a proper perspective on healing and deliverance ministry as practiced by Christ and subsequent followers, we will examine the healing and deliverance methods that Jesus and early Christians used. Additionally, we will define healing and deliverance (exorcism). It is important to understand that the words *deliverance* and *exorcism* are in essence interchangeable terms used to describe the ministry process of removing demonic oppression from an individual. We will then look at examples of healing and deliverance ministry throughout church history to the present. The section will conclude with a closing statement about the practice of Christian healing during these periods and the validity of this ministry for today.

---

3 Keener, *Miracles*, 1:390. Cf. Candy Gunther Brown, *Global Pentecostal and Charismatic Healing* (New York: Oxford University Press, 2011), 29–45.

4 Cf. Kelsey, *Healing and Christianity*,154–173; Keener, *Miracles*, 1:366–371 for a discussion of healing during the Middle Ages. For more on Hume and the Enlightenment, see Keener, *Miracles*, 1:107–210.

5 Cf. Keener, *Miracles*; Brown, *Global* for extended documentation of healing and miracle accounts in the twentieth and twenty-first centuries.

The Kingdom Model for Healing and Deliverance

Our Christian history reflects a rich heritage of God working through the church in healing, deliverance (exorcism), and other *charisms* of the Spirit. From the gospel accounts to modern times, God still heals the sick and delivers the oppressed through ordinary Christians who understand that the gospel of the kingdom is not only one of love and of the Word, but also one of power and demonstration in the Spirit.[6] Many consider healing and deliverance to be outside the realm of orthodox Christianity, when both the New Testament and Christian history record these graces as part of normative Christianity. As Keener states, "Luke is clearly convinced that miracles occur; Paul is likewise convinced that they happened during his ministry (Rom 15:19; 2 Cor 12:12). Modern scholars are also usually convinced that Jesus and many early Christians (e.g., second-century exorcists) were believed to perform miracles."[7]

We see Jesus throughout the Gospels demonstrating the kingdom of God by healing the sick, casting out demons, and performing miracles. The gospel of the kingdom was one of power that healed the sick and delivered the oppressed. Gary S. Greig states that "alongside preaching, Jesus' healing and casting out demons was His primary means of proclaiming the gospel of God's Kingdom, and New Testament scholars around the world have recognized this for decades."[8] According to Keener, "Most scholars

---

6 1 Cor 2:4–5; 4:20. Cf. Keener, *Miracles*; Brown, *Global* for extended documentation of current healing and miracle accounts.

7 Keener, *Miracles*, 1:33.

8 Gary S. Greig. "Power Evangelism: Learning to Depend on the Holy Spirit, His Healing, His Gifts, & His Power to Follow the Pattern of Jesus Kingdom Ministry," (2003):14, http://www.cwgministries.org/books/Power-Evangelism.pdf.

recognize that in the Gospels, Jesus' miracles function as signs of the kingdom (also Mt 12:28//Lk 11:20)."[9]

After demonstrating this model of ministry to the disciples, Jesus empowered them to do the same: "Then Jesus summoned his twelve disciples and gave them authority over unclean spirits, to cast them out, and to cure every disease and every sickness" (Mt 10:1 NRSV). He commanded them to go, preach, heal, cast out demons, cleanse lepers, and raise the dead as the occasion might demand (cf. Mt 10:7–8; Lk 9:1–2). After his resurrection, he commissioned the disciples to make disciples of all the nations, teaching them to observe all that they were instructed (cf. Mt 28:18–20). Jesus instructed those disciples to teach others what they were taught and commanded previously. What were they taught? The disciples were taught how to heal the sick, cast out demons, and proclaim the gospel of the kingdom in power, not just in word. This was normal Christian ministry for the early church, and Christ intended it to be common ministry practice for all who would believe and follow him. Borobio believes that "the *charism* of healing should be understood as forming part of an integral element in the overall mission. This is an 'unequal' but true, at once historical and prophetic, anamnetic and charismatic, mission and continuation of Christ's complete ministry to the sick."[10] Jesus deliberately taught his disciples in this kingdom ministry model. According to Keener, "Perhaps Jesus even deliberately trained his disciples as his successors, as teachers normally trained their disciples to be, expecting them to be able to perform the same activity that he did (cf. Mk 9:18–19, 28–29; 11:23; Lk 9:40–41; 17:6)."[11] According to Kelsey, "It is also clear that Jesus sent his disciples out to continue

---

9 Keener, *Miracles*, 1:61. See his footnote for extensive source citations to substantiate this statement.

10 Borobio, "Enquiry into Healing," 38.

11 Keener, *Miracles*, 1:29.

this basic ministry (Mk 6:7–13; Mt 10:5–10; Lk 9:1–6). The book of Acts records how well they carried out this commission. It is difficult to see how [Rudolf] Bultmann, and many who follow him, can eliminate this entire ministry on theological and philosophical grounds by calling it mythology."[12]

From the day of Pentecost to present day, followers of Christ who have believed and practiced this kingdom model of ministry have continued the work of Christ by proclaiming the gospel, healing the sick, and freeing the demonized. This model was extremely effective and necessary for the advancement of the church in the first three centuries. While the Christian apologists and writers such as Justin Martyr and Tertullian made significant inroads into Greco-Roman culture with their polemics, it was the healings, exorcisms, caring for the poor, and tenacious faith of those early Christians (despite the ridicule, persecution, and martyrdom they faced) that had the most impact on the advancement of the church.[13] Early church father Athanasius, bishop of Alexandria (AD 296–298), in writing about the Life of Antony, confirms the inadequacy of argument alone to convince people of the Christian message by stating, "We however make our proof not in the persuasive words of Greek wisdom as our teacher has it, but we persuade by the faith which manifestly precedes argumentative proof," and he went on to demonstrate the Christian message by casting out demons from some who were standing by.[14] Keener adds to this thought by stating that demonstration substantiates the message

---

12 Kelsey, *Healing and Christianity*, 43.

13 Cf. Kelsey, *Healing and Christianity*, 103–156; MacMullen, *Christianizing the Roman Empire passim*; Keener, *Miracles*, 1:35–82.

14 Athanasius, *The Life of Antony*, 80, http://www.newadvent.org/fathers/2811.htm.

delivered: "Patristic sources continued to use miracles and particularly exorcisms as proofs verifying their claims."[15]

According to Ramsey MacMullen, professor emeritus of History at Yale University, and author of *Christianizing the Roman Empire (AD 100–400)*, the primary reason that nonbelievers came to Christ in the Roman Empire during the early centuries of the faith was mainly a result of witnessing the Christians performing miracles (i.e., expelling demons and healing the sick).[16] MacMullen states concerning miracles, "Miracles further served as a proof, not only of a divine authority behind Christian teachings, but as proof of God's unique claim to his title, whereas other supernatural beings deserved only to be called *daimones*."[17]

Despite the political forces arrayed against Christianity during the early centuries, the church continued to grow at considerable rates, primarily due to the care of the sick during epidemics.[18] Irenaeus, bishop of Lyons, France (AD 120–202), who was discipled by Polycarp (who was believed to be discipled by the Apostle John), provides insight into the evangelical nature of exorcisms and healings:

> Those who are in truth His disciples, receiving grace from Him, do in His name perform [miracles], so as to promote the welfare of other men, according to the gift which each one has received from Him. For some do certainly and truly drive out devils, so that those who have thus been cleansed from evil spirits frequently both believe [in Christ], and

---

15 Keener, *Miracles*, 1:62.

16 MacMullen, *Christianizing the Roman Empire*, 108.

17 Ibid.

18 Porterfield, *Healing*, 50. Porterfield states, "Despite the considerable political force exerted to suppress Christianity, sociologist Rodney Stark attributed its remarkable growth in the second and third centuries to the extreme altruism of Christians who attended the sick during epidemics."

join themselves to the Church. Others have foreknowledge of things to come: they see visions, and utter prophetic expressions. Others still, heal the sick by laying their hands upon them, and they are made whole. Yea, moreover, as I have said, the dead even have been raised up, and remained among us for many years.[19]

William L. De Arteaga, PhD, an Anglican priest and author who is known internationally as a Christian historian and expert on the rebirth and renewal of the Christian healing movement, comments, "Irenaeus' accent on the healing/exorcism ministry of the Early Church as having evangelical consequences has escaped serious attention by modern scholars, who often have an anti-supernatural prejudice."[20] As we will develop more in a following section, the rapid rise of Christianity in the early centuries can clearly be traced to the mission and model of kingdom ministry demonstrated first by Christ and then continued by his disciples.

Defining Christian Healing and Deliverance

Christian healing, foundationally explained, is accomplished through the name of Christ and by the power of the Holy Spirit through a variety of spiritual and practical methods. Christian healing may also involve repentance and forgiveness of sin, frequently with the act of forgiveness releasing healing for the individual.

---

19 Irenaeus of Lyons, "Irenæus against Heresies," in *The Ante-Nicene Fathers, Volume I: The Apostolic Fathers With Justin Martyr and Irenaeus*, ed. Alexander Roberts, James Donaldson and A. Cleveland Coxe (Buffalo, NY: Christian Literature Company, 1885), 409.

20 William L. De Arteaga, *Forging a Renewed Hebraic and Pauline Christianity* (Unpublished Manuscript: 2011), 14.

Christian healing could be defined as the divine interaction of God through Christ by the power of the Holy Spirit to accelerate the healing of physical, emotional, or psychological conditions of an individual as a result of prayer, the laying on of hands, anointing with oil, sacraments, liturgy, confession, repentance, or *charism* of the Spirit. While God's healing power is also achieved through the aid of nurses, physicians, and hospitals, healing through medical practice is not the primary focus of this book. Rather, accounts of healing and deliverance as God's people minister to those in need as a result of the abovementioned spiritual practices shall be examined.

As previously noted in the biblical basis for healing in Section One, one of the earliest practices of caring for the sick was derived from James: "Are any among you sick? They should call for the elders of the church and have them pray over them, anointing them with oil in the name of the Lord. The prayer of faith will save the sick, and the Lord will raise them up; and anyone who has committed sins will be forgiven" (Jas 5:14–15 NRSV). In this passage, James reveals aspects of a healing model that the early church frequently used: prayer over the person combined with anointing him or her with oil in the name of Christ.

When observing the ministry of Jesus, the gospel accounts often link deliverance (exorcism) with healing: "That evening they brought to him many who were possessed with demons; and he cast out the spirits with a word, and cured all who were sick. This was to fulfill what had been spoken through the prophet Isaiah, 'He took our infirmities and bore our diseases'" (Mt 8:16–17 NRSV). In a similar manner, when the early church prayed for the sick, exorcism and healing were frequently associated. Once the demons were removed, healing often occurred immediately in the individual receiving prayer. Kelsey states, "Since both bodily and mental illnesses were a sign of domination by some evil entity, the power to heal disease was prime evidence that the opposite spirit, the Spirit of God, was operating through the healer. Thus the healing of 'demon possession' was often spoken of in conjunction with curing illness from other causes."[21]

Avery Brook, author of *Plain Prayers in a Complicated World* and *Finding God*, describes how the early church developed elaborate healing and deliverance models:

> In due course, special services of healing were developed with laying on of hands and anointing with oil. These services could become quite elaborate. Several priests and laity visited the sick person at home. They started by exorcising and blessing the house. Then the sick person knelt for the laying on of hands. He was anointed on the throat, breast, and back, and more liberally where the pain was greatest. Prayers of thanksgiving were made, the patient was told to pray for his own recovery and to make his confession. The Eucharist then followed. This group of priests and laity—or part of it—came back every week until the person was well.[22]

Many of the Patristic fathers wrote of the link between healing and exorcism as performed by ordinary Christians. For example, Justin Martyr, an early Christian apologist (AD 100–165), in his Second Apology to the emperor in Rome records, "For numberless demoniacs throughout the whole world, and in your city, many of our Christian men exorcising them in the name of Jesus Christ…have healed and do heal, rendering helpless and driving the possessing devils out of the men, though they could not be cured by all

---

21 Kelsey, *Healing and Christianity*, 118–119.
22 Avery Brooke, "Christian Healing in History," *Weavings* 6 (1991): 9.

the other exorcists, and those who used incantations and drugs."[23] Notice how Justin intertwines healing and exorcism in his argument to the Roman Senate, implying that the healing is a result of the exorcism.

In this book, the word *deliverance* is used instead of *exorcism* or *casting out of demons*, although many references cited may use these terms to describe the removal of demonic spirits from an individual. The English definition for *exorcism* is to "drive out (a supposed evil spirit) from a person or place."[24] The English definition of *deliverance* is "the process of being rescued or set free."[25] I define *deliverance* simply as the expulsion or exorcism of evil spirits from an individual by freeing people from demonic oppression through the name and authority of Christ and by the power of the Holy Spirit (cf. Mk 16:17–18). Candy Gunther Brown, professor of Religious Studies at Indiana University Bloomington, further clarifies by stating, "Although the term 'exorcism' can properly be used to refer to efforts (most of which are not dramatic) to cast out evil spirits, the alternative terms 'deliverance' or 'liberation,'… underline the priority for participants of freeing individuals from oppression rather than focusing on the demons themselves."[26] Additionally, many may be demonized (oppressed) but are not necessarily possessed—in which case the use of the word *deliverance* is more applicable and humane to the one receiving ministry.

---

23 Justin Martyr, "The Second Apology of Justin," in *The Ante-Nicene Fathers, Volume I: The Apostolic Fathers With Justin Martyr and Irenaeus*, ed. Alexander Roberts, James Donaldson, and A. Cleveland Coxe (Buffalo, NY: Christian Literature Company, 1885), 190. Citing from 6.

24 C. Soanes and A. Stevenson, *Concise Oxford English Dictionary*, 11th ed. (Oxford, UK: Oxford University Press, 2004).

25 Ibid.

26 Brown, *Global*, 5.

Chapter 8

HEALING AND DELIVERANCE DURING THE PATRISTIC PERIOD

During the Patristic period, healings, deliverance, and miracles appear to be the normative practice and primary evangelistic tool of the early church. Preaching the gospel of Christ was frequently accompanied by demonstrations of God's power to heal and deliver the oppressed. According to Keener, "Second- and third-century Christian apologists depict not only apostolic leaders but also ordinary Christians as miracle workers."[1] Eusebius, bishop of Caesarea in the early fourth century and known as the "Father of Church History," records that many "preached the

---

1 Keener, *Miracles*, 1:362.

Gospel more and more widely and scattered the saving seeds of the kingdom of heaven far and near throughout the whole world,"[2] and functioning as evangelists, with God's grace and power, witnessed "a great many wonderful works...done through them by the power of the divine Spirit, so that at the first hearing whole multitudes of men eagerly embraced the religion of the Creator of the universe."[3]

Origen, a third-century theologian in the Eastern Church, in his treatise *Against Celsus,* writes openly of healing and deliverance among the early church: "They expel evil spirits, and perform many cures, and foresee certain events, according to the will of the Logos."[4] In defending the name of Christ, Origen adds, "And the name of Jesus can still remove distractions from the minds of men, and expel demons, and also take away diseases."[5] Amanda Porterfield says of Origen, "In the third century, Origen had championed the idea that Christ was the 'great physician,' along with the idea that bishops and other representatives of Christ were 'physicians of souls.'"[6] Ignatius, bishop of Antioch during the early second century, proclaimed, "'There is only one physician, first subject to suffering and then beyond it, Jesus Christ our Lord.'"[7] Keener states, "Reports continued among early church fa-

---

2 Eusebius of Caesaria, "Church History," trans. Arthur Cushman McGiffert, in *A Select Library of the Nicene and Post-Nicene Fathers of the Christian Church, Second Series, Volume I: Eusebius: Church History, Life of Constantine the Great, and Oration in Praise of Constantine,* ed. Philip Schaff and Henry Wace (New York: Christian Literature Company, 1890), 169. Citing from 3.37.

3 Ibid.

4 Origen, "Origen against Celsus," trans. Frederick Crombie, in *The Ante-Nicene Fathers, Volume IV: Fathers of the Third Century: Tertullian, Part Fourth; Minucius Felix; Commodian; Origen, Parts First and Second,* ed. Alexander Roberts, James Donaldson, and A. Cleveland Coxe (Buffalo, NY: Christian Literature Company, 1885), 415. Citing from 1.46.

5 Origen, 427, citing from 1.67.

6 Porterfield, *Healing,* 53.

7 Ignatius, *To the Ephesians,* quoted in Porterfield, *Healing,* 44.

thers like Basil and Gregory of Nazianzus, Gregory of Nyssa, John Chrysostom, and also among the desert monks."[8] The early church saw Christ as both the savior for our sins and as the physician and healer for humanity. Furthermore, they fully believed and expected that the healing ministry of Christ was active through God's church by the power of the Holy Spirit. According to Keener, "Far from being merely incredulous about a distant and unverifiable past, various church fathers noted that miracles and healings continued in their own day."[9]

Cyprian, bishop of Carthage and an important Christian writer in the third century, speaks of Christ's power to heal in the sacraments, and states that deliverance was a normal aspect of the sacrament of baptism for believers: "This, finally, in very fact also we experience, that those who are baptized by urgent necessity in sickness, and obtain grace, are free from the unclean spirit wherewith they were previously moved, and live in the Church in praise and honor, and day by day make more and more advance in the increase of heavenly grace by the growth of their faith."[10] Cyprian adds concerning deliverance, "When they are adjured by us in the name of the true God, yield forthwith, and confess, and admit they are forced also to leave the bodies they have invaded."[11]

Tertullian, a Christian apologist considered the "Father of Latin Christianity" in the second and third centuries, was bold in declaring the authority a Christian has over demons: "Let a man be produced right here before your court who, it is clear, is possessed

---

8 Keener, *Miracles*, 1:363.

9 Ibid., 1:362.

10 Cyprian of Carthage, "The Epistles of Cyprian," trans. Robert Ernest Wallis, in *The Ante-Nicene Fathers, Volume V: Fathers of the Third Century: Hippolytus, Cyprian, Novatian, Appendix*, ed. Alexander Roberts, James Donaldson, and A. Cleveland Coxe (Buffalo, NY: Christian Literature Company, 1886), 402. Citing from 75.16.

11 MacMullen, *Christianizing the Roman Empire*, 27.

by a demon, and that spirit, commanded by any Christian at all, will as much confess himself a demon in truth as, by lying, he will elsewhere profess himself a 'god.'"[12] To the proconsul of North Africa, Tertullian mentions specific cases of healing and deliverance by the Christians: "The clerk of one of them who was liable to be thrown upon the ground by an evil spirit, was set free from his affliction; as was also the relative of another, and the little boy of a third. How many men of rank (to say nothing of common people) have been delivered from devils, and healed of diseases!"[13]

One of the compelling evidences for the pagans of the Roman Empire to become Christian was the ability of these early believers to heal the sick and exorcise demons. Irenaeus, in his effort to defend the incarnation of Christ and refute Gnosticism, discusses how the Christians continued the same works of Christ. As mentioned earlier in this book, Irenaeus describes the normality of healing and deliverance in the church in his treatise *Against Heresies*:

> Wherefore also those who are in truth His disciples receiving grace from Him do in His name perform miracles so as to promote the welfare of other men according to the gift which each one has received from Him. For some do certainly and truly drive out devils so that those who have thus been cleansed from evil spirits frequently both believe in Christ and join themselves to the church. Others have foreknowledge of things to come they see visions and utter prophetic expressions. Others still heal the sick by laying their hands upon them and they are made whole. Yea moreover as I have said the dead even have been raised up

---

12 MacMullen, *Christianizing the Roman Empire*, 27.

13 Tertullian, "To Scapula," trans. S. Thelwall, in *The Ante-Nicene Fathers, Volume III: Latin Christianity: Its Founder, Tertullian*, ed. Alexander Roberts, James Donaldson, and A. Cleveland Coxe (Buffalo, NY: Christian Literature Company, 1885), 107. Citing 4.

and remained among us for many years. And what shall I more say? It is not possible to name the number of the gifts which the church scattered throughout the whole world has received from God in the name of Jesus Christ.[14]

In this dialogue, Irenaeus presents a list of *charisms* on par with what is observed in the Gospels and Acts, and the subsequent effect of these signs in converting unbelievers to Christ. [15] Irenaeus, as well as other early church leaders, used healings and exorcisms in apologetics to defend the Christian movement.[16]

Athanasius, the bishop of Alexandria in Egypt during the fourth century, is best known for refuting Arianism during the council of Nicaea. Athanasius writes of the healings witnessed by his friend Antony:

Such are the words of Antony, and we ought not to doubt whether such marvels were wrought by the hand of a man. For it is the promise of the Saviour, when He says, "If you have faith as a grain of mustard seed, you shall say to this mountain, remove hence and it shall remove; and nothing shall be impossible unto you Matthew 17:20." And again, "Verily, verily, I say unto you, if you shall ask the father in My name He will give it you. Ask and you shall receive John 16:23." And He himself it is who says to His disciples and to all who believe in Him, "Heal the sick, cast out demons; freely you have received, freely give Matthew 10:8." Antony, at any rate, healed not by commanding, but by prayer and speaking the name of Christ. So that it was clear to all that

---

14 Irenaeus, 2.32.4.

15 Keener, *Miracles*, 1:363; cf. Kelsey, *Healing and Christianity*, 150–51.

16 Ibid.

it was not he himself who worked, but the Lord who showed mercy by his means and healed the sufferers.[17]

Athanasius describes Antony as a Christian who healed and delivered many who came to him, demonstrating the very doctrine affirmed at Nicaea in AD 325 that "Christ was both man and God, and that Christ extended his divine power, which was his by nature as God's son, through his adopted saints and their healing work."[18]

By the fifth century, Augustine, bishop of Hippo and early Christian theologian whose writings influenced the development of Western Christianity, began to take a theological position that healing and miracles were no longer operative in his time. His stance against the necessity of healing and miracles affected the church for centuries, although he changed his view later in life. Augustine states, "These miracles are not allowed to continue into our time, lest the soul should always require things that can always be seen, and by becoming accustomed to them mankind should grow cold towards the very thing whose novelty had made men glow with fire."[19] Later in life, as Augustine neared the completion of *The City of God*, he shifted his theological view in favor of the ministry of healing and deliverance, admitting that he had been wrong.[20] Augustine, in the final section of his work, begins to record and attest to the numerous miracles taking place in his region. He admits that he cannot record all of the miracles, but does attest to seventy miracles during a two-year span: "I am so pressed by the promise of finishing this work, that I cannot record all the miracles I know....For when I saw, in our own times,

---

17 Athanasius, *Antony*, 83–84.

18 Porterfield, *Healing*, 63–64.

19 Augustine, *De Vera Religione*, 25. 46–47, quoted in Kelsey, *Healing and Christianity*, 146.

20 Kelsey, *Healing and Christianity*, 145.

frequent signs of the presence of divine powers similar to those which had been given of old, I desired that narratives might be written,...It is not yet two years...almost seventy at the hour at which I write."[21] Augustine adds, "Even now, therefore, many miracles are wrought, the same God who wrought those we read of still performing them, by whom He will and as He will."[22] Keener notes that "Augustine's many examples of miracles of which he was certain include dramatic cases like healing of long-term paralytics; he freely cites eyewitnesses. Sometimes he expresses his annoyance when someone healed had not yet publically given testimony to what God had done."[23] While Augustine eventually repudiated his cessationist position, his earlier cessationist views no doubt affected some in his own time, as he complained that miracles were relatively unknown due to suppressed communication and the conditioned unbelief of the people.[24]

---

21 Augustine, *The City of God*, 22.8, http://www.fordham.edu/halsall/source/augustine-cityofgod-22-9-10.asp.

22 Ibid.

23 Keener, *Miracles*, 1:365.

24 Ruthven, *Cessation*, 18.

Chapter 9

Healing and Deliverance during the Middle Ages, AD 500–1500

As mentioned with Augustine, there were many church leaders toward the end of the Patristic period who began to adopt a cessationist view toward the *charisms* of the Spirit, including healing and deliverance.[1] Keener writes of this period, "Healing reports continued, though their typical character shifted further from what we find in our earliest Christian sources."[2] According to Ruthven, this doctrinal view became prevalent in the Middle Ages, as many church leaders believed "the role of the devout is no longer to expect miracles, but to pursue virtues prescribed in church Scriptures and doctrines."[3] Ruthven further comments, "Prophecy became preaching or teaching, or the various miracles of healing became metaphors for regeneration: the 'blind' see the light of the Gospel, the 'lame' walk the paths of righteousness, the 'dead' are raised to newness of life."[4]

---

1 Prior to and since Augustine, cessationist proponents have argued the discontinuance of the gifts of the Spirit, claiming that the *charismata* of the Spirit (i.e., prophetic revelation, gifts of healing, or the miraculous) are no longer in operation today, or at best in a diminished state. See De Arteaga, *Forging*, 68, "This belief, that miracles and the healing ministry ceased after biblical times is called 'cessationism.' In this view the purpose of miracles was to authenticate the authority of an Old Testament prophet, or Jesus and His apostles. Missing in the cessationist theology of miracles is an understanding of healing as a sign of God's compassion or the miraculous as a mark of the Kingdom (see Mk 8:2, Lk 9:1-2). The idea of cessationism originated well before Augustine. It can be traced to Jewish rabbinical commentaries that preceded the Christian era. Some rabbis were concerned that since the times of Haggai, Zechariah and Malachi there had not been an authentic prophet in Israel. Several ideas were proposed to explain why this was so, such as the lack of piety among the population." Cf. Ruthven, *Cessation*, xxii, "Cessationism, then, is not simply an odd, tolerable doctrine of traditional theology. It strikes at the very heart of biblical revelation—at the core message of the Bible: that the normative pattern for God and man is the goal of immediate, direct revelation as the essential part of the intimate, divinely-ordained relationship, so that 'I will be their God and they shall be my people' (Jer 31:33)."

2 Keener, *Miracles*, 1:366.

3 Ruthven, *Cessation*, 20.

4 Ibid., 19. Cf. Ruthven footnote: "On the Christian tradition of spiritualizing of miracles see, e.g., Origen, *Against Celsus*, 1.46; 2.48, 42, 94; similarly Augustine, *Sermons on the Selected Lessons of the New Testament*, 38.3 (NPF, 1st ser., IV, p. 379): 'The blind body does not now open its eyes by a miracle of the Lord, but the blinded heart opens its eyes to the world of the Lord. The physical corpse does not now rise again, but the soul rises again which lies dead in a living body. The deaf ears of the body are not now opened; but how many who have the ears of their hearts closed, let them fly open at the penetrating word of God.' This metaphorical treatment of miracles led easily to Bultmann's program of demythologization."

Gregory the Great, an influential Pope (AD 540–604), took a cessationist position that the miracles were necessary at the beginning of the church age in order for faith and the church to grow, but once the church was established, miracles began to diminish.[5] Unfortunately, many like Gregory began to rationalize the lack of healing, deliverance, and miracles that were once common in the early church and Patristic period.[6] According to Kelsey, sickness and disease that was once viewed as a result of demonic spirits and afflictions to be confronted through the victory of Christ was now believed to be a "mark of God's correction, sometimes inflicted by the negative powers with divine approval, to bring moral renewal."[7] Gregory and others began to see sickness as a means to bring the sinner to a place of contrition for his or her sins. It was the righteous who would find healing, not the unrepentant.

With disasters and plagues sweeping Europe during the sixth and seventh centuries, sickness began to be understood by the church as God's displeasure with humanity rather than the church viewing, as seen in the New Testament, God's love and desire to heal humanity as displayed through the life of Christ and his followers. The sacrament of healing transitioned from healing the sick to an emphasis upon unction for dying, with the focus directed toward preparation for eternity.[8] According to De Arteaga, "Theodult of Orleans (Bishop of Orleans from AD 798–818) proposed that the

---

5 Ruthven, *Cessation*, 18–19. See Gregory the Great, *Homily on the Gospels*, 29, PL, 76, col. 1215, quoted in Ruthven, *Cessation*, 18–19, "These things [miracles described in Mk 16:17–18] were necessary in the beginning of the church, for in order that faith might grow, it had to be nourished by miracles; for we, too, when we plant shrubs, pour water on them till we see that they have gotten a strong hold on the ground; and when once they are firmly rooted, we stopped the watering. For this reason Paul says; 'Tongues are for a sign, not to believers, but to unbelievers.'"

6 Ibid.

7 Kelsey, *Healing and Christianity*, 1:155.

8 Ibid., 1:159, 163.

main function of the sacrament of anointing the sick was to impart a 'sanctifying grace.' This grace supplemented the grace of the sacrament of penance."[9] Anointing with oil and prayer for the sick became anointing for last rites and preparation for death, promising the sick to go straight to heaven and avoid purgatory should they die. Theodult declared, "When the sick man has been anointed in the way that has been set forth, let him be enjoined by the priest to say the Lord's Prayer and the Creed, and to commend his spirit into the hands of God, and to fortify himself with the sign of the cross, and to bid farewell to the living."[10]

Instead of believers functioning from the *charisms* in the Apostolic Church (i.e., Church of the Great Commission in Mt 28), healing and deliverance ministry became associated with isolated mystical saints who predominately adopted a monastic lifestyle. Considering the impact Gregory the Great had upon the Western Church and Roman Catholicism, his views were far-reaching for centuries. Despite Gregory's, and other church leaders', pessimistic view of healing as fostered in the Middle Ages, he promoted

---

9 De Arteaga, *Forging*, 72.
10 Ibid., 73.

healing and recorded many miracles during this era, including the raising of the dead.[11]

Gregory also recorded healings and miracles performed through Benedict in his *Dialogues*. Benedict established one of the first monasteries in the Western Church in Monte Cassino in AD 529, and developed *The Rule of Benedict* that provided a principal framework for monastic life and work for many years. Gregory tells an account of Benedict raising a fellow monk from the dead, who had fallen during a construction project. He writes,

> The man of God was in his room at the time, praying, when the Devil appeared to him and remarked sarcastically that he was on his way to visit the brethren at their work. Benedict quickly sent them word to be on their guard against the evil spirit who would soon be with them. Just as they received his

---

11 Saint Gregory the Great, *Dialogues*, translated by Odo John Zimmerman, *The Fathers of the Church* (New York: Fathers of the Church, 1959), 48–49, "'In the same city of Todi,' he began, 'there was a man of exemplary life named Marcellus, who lived there with his two sisters. On Holy Saturday evening he took sick and died. Since it was necessary to carry his remains a great distance, he could not be buried the same day. The consequent delay in the funeral services gave the two sisters time to hurry to their revered bishop, Fortunatus, and pour out their hearts in grief. "We know that you follow in the footsteps of the holy Apostles," they said, "and that you cleanse lepers and give sight to the blind. Come with us and bring our brother back to life." This was very sad news for Bishop Fortunatus and he, too, could not restrain his tears. "Go home again," he told them, "and do not insist on this request of yours, for your brother's death occurred by God's decree, which no man can oppose." With this answer the two sisters departed, leaving the bishop to mourn his friend's death. Before dawn of Easter Sunday he summoned his two deacons and went with them to the home of the deceased, proceeding directly to the place where the corpse was laid out. There he knelt down and after praying for some time rose and sat down near the body. Then in a subdued voice he called, "Brother Marcellus." At the sound of this low voice so near him, the dead man was roused as though awakened from a gentle slumber. Opening his eyes and looking at the bishop, he said, "What have you done? What have you done?" The bishop in turn asked, "What have I done?" To this Marcellus answered: "Yesterday two people came to release me from the body and lead me to the abode of the blessed. Today a messenger is sent to them with the command, 'Take him back, because Bishop Fortunatus is visiting at his home.'" Marcellus quickly regained his strength and lived a long time after this episode.'"

warning, the Devil overturned the wall, crushing under its ruins the body of a very young monk who was the son of a tax collector. Unconcerned about the damaged wall in their grief and dismay over the loss of their brother, the monks hurried to Abbot Benedict to let him know of the dreadful accident. He told them to bring the mangled body to his room. It had to be carried in on a blanket, for the wall had not only broken the boy's arms and legs but had crushed all the bones in his body. The saint had the remains placed on the reed matting where he used to pray and after that told them all to leave. Then he closed the door and knelt down to offer his most earnest prayers to God. That very hour, to the astonishment of all, he sent the boy back to his work as sound and healthy as he had been before. Thus, in spite of the Devil's attempt to mock the man of God by causing this tragic death, the young monk was able to rejoin his brethren and help them finish the wall. Meanwhile, Benedict began to manifest the spirit of prophecy by foretelling future events and by describing to those who were with him what they had done in his absence.[12]

Gregory also describes an account of deliverance performed by Benedict as he simply struck the monk on the cheek: "The evil spirit had entered one of the older monks whom he found drawing water and had thrown him to the ground in a violent convulsion. When the man of God caught sight of this old brother in such torment, he merely struck him on the cheek, and the evil spirit was promptly driven out, never to return."[13] Gregory records many other miracles performed by Benedict in his *Dialogues*, and it is

---

12 Gregory, *Dialogues*, 76–77.
13 Ibid., 98.

fascinating to read the normalcy with which this brother operated in healings, deliverance, and miracles.

Similar to Benedict, we see in the life of seventh-century monk Cuthbert a similar pattern of healings, deliverance, and miracles. He became quite celebrated for the numerous miracles that he performed, in particular the deliverances. Charles, the Archbishop of Glasgow, writes that Cuthbert, "by the earnestness of his prayers, restored to their former health many that were afflicted with various infirmities and sufferings; some that were troubled by unclean spirits, he not only cured whilst present, by touching them, praying over them, or even by commanding or exorcising the devils to go out of them, but even when absent he restored them by his prayers, or by foretelling that they should be restored."[14]

Kelsey states that along with Cuthbert in England during the seventh century, there were "eyewitness accounts of healings by the saintly John of Beverly, who was bishop of York until he retired to found a monastery. John healed the wife of an earl, as well as a man dying after a fall from his horse."[15] Porterfield likens a sixth-century deliverance and subsequent healing of a young man who was deaf and mute by a man known as a healer, Saint Hospicius, as an indication that the central ministry of Christ and the early Christians had been carried forward into the Middle Ages. Porterfield states that through this miracle, Hospicius "replicated one of the cures ascribed to Jesus in the gospels (Mk 7:31–37; cf.

---

14 Charles, Archbishop of Glasgow, *The History of St. Cuthbert* (New York: Catholic Publication Society Co., 1887), 28–29.

15 Kelsey, *Healing and Christianity*, 180.

Mt 15:29–31) and carried forward the rite of exorcism that was a conspicuous part of early Christianity."[16]

Benedict, Cuthbert, Hospicius, and others during the Middle Ages were simply following in the footsteps of Christ and the early church. Healings, deliverances, and miracles were normative during the ministry of Christ and the early church, and they continued through this period. According to Keener, "The Eastern churches also continued to report healings, for example, in Constantinople and Ethiopia."[17] In later centuries of the Middle Ages, other notable healing accounts are recorded. Some reported healings after Anselm blessed the Eucharist; many other healings were linked to Dominic, founder of the Dominican order, and St. Francis of Assisi.[18] Kelsey states, "Indeed, St. Francis had to be buried hurriedly to keep his body from being dismembered by people who wanted even the smallest relic which still carried the healing power he had in life."[19]

Like Augustine toward the end of the Patristic period and Gregory the Great in the beginning of the Middle Ages, Thomas Aquinas, an influential philosopher and theologian in the tradition of scholasticism in the thirteenth century, began to steer

---

16 Porterfield, *Healing*, 67–68. Porterfield writes of this story, "In *The History of the Franks* (c. 592), Gregory of Tours described a healer outside of Nice with 'iron chains wound round his body, next to the skin,' and 'a hair-shirt on top.' For most of the year, the healer, Hospicius, 'ate nothing but dry bread and a few dates.' 'Through the agency of this holy man,' according to Gregory, 'the Lord deigned to perform remarkable miracles,' including the restoration of hearing and speech to a young man struck deaf and dumb during a fever...Thus, in casting out the demon causing the young man's loss of hearing and speech, Hospicius in using oil as part of a simple but forceful procedure to expel demons followed in the path of bishops, deacons, and lay exorcists in early churches who used oil to exorcise and heal the sick, and also emulated the disciples who, under the commission from Jesus, 'cast out many demons, and anointed with oil many who were sick and cured them' (Mk 6:13; cf. Mt 10:1; Lk 9:1)."

17 Keener, *Miracles*, 1:370. See footnotes for further discussion.

18 Kelsey, *Healing and Christianity*, 181–182.

19 Ibid.

the church away from the belief and practice of healing and deliverance to a theology that was more rationalistic and pessimistic toward this ministry. Aquinas did acknowledge and believe in miracles, but his theology largely saw the miracles of Christ as a means of proving the Christian faith and church doctrine.[20] Clark states, "It was a theology based on the senses and ability to reason, and left little room for the supernatural as it pertained to earthly life. His writing (Aquinas) became the benchmark of church theology for the next several hundred years."[21] Ruthven adds regarding Aquinas, "Thomas Aquinas ordered the pattern of cessationist tenets which dominated the church until the 20th century."[22]

Aquinas embraced Gregory the Great's view concerning the gifts of the Holy Spirit; namely, that wisdom, science, understanding, counsel, fortitude, piety, and fear replaced the healing, miracles, prophecy, and other gifts of the Holy Spirit mentioned by Paul in 1 Cor 12.[23] Kelsey makes these observations regarding Aquinas's view of the Holy Spirit gifts as expressed in his *Summa Theologica*: "Aquinas had no real place for religious healing in his systematic thought, and his basic ideas gradually gained acceptance among Protestant thinkers as well as Catholic theologians. It is impossible to understand the intellectual rejection of the healing ministry in modern times without following his reasoning closely."[24] Kelsey continues concerning Aquinas, "These gifts, he held, were the perfections that disposed human beings 'to be moved by God' (II–I.68.1) toward 'the Divine good which is known by the intellect

---

20 Ruthven, *Cessation*, 21.

21 Randy Clark, *There Is More: Reclaiming the Power of Impartation* (Mechanicsburg, PA: Global Awakening, 2006), 70.

22 Ruthven, *Cessation*, 20. Cf. his footnote for more on the influence of Aquinas in later Christian thought concerning miracles.

23 Kelsey, *Healing and Christianity*, 170.

24 Ibid., 167, 170.

alone' (II–II.24.1)....The real purpose of these gifts was to produce an effective teacher, for one could only lead another person to God by instructing him (II–I.111.4)." [25]

The early church saw its rapid growth through a gospel of the kingdom preached and demonstrated with healings, deliverance, and miracles as normative. By the time of Aquinas in the Middle Ages, reason and intellectual teaching became the predominate focus, rather than demonstrating the gospel of Christ in word and in power (1 Cor 4:20). Despite this, God continued to heal and deliver the demonized through ordinary people (although frequently called saints) who made themselves available to this ministry. We now transition to the Reformation period, where, despite a continuing negative trend toward healing and deliverance ministry, it was still practiced and observed.

---

25 Kelsey, *Healing and Christianity*, 167, 170.

Chapter 10

Healing and Deliverance during the Reformation, AD 1500–1750

In 1517, Martin Luther posted his Ninety-Five Theses on the door of the church in Wittenberg, beginning the Reformation. Luther, Calvin, Zwingli, and other Reformers fought to restore the Roman Catholic Church to an adherence upon scripture alone, *sola scriptura*, by grace alone, *sola gratia*, by faith alone, *sola fide*, and by Christ alone, *sola Christi*.[1] They were deeply troubled by the abusive practices of the church, primarily the teachings of purgatory, the related practice of selling indulgences, and traffic in inauthentic relics.[2] In their effort to restore the church to orthodoxy, the Reformers predominately opposed the miraculous and healing nature of the gospel of Christ, seeking to reform or

---

1 Ruthven, *What's Wrong*, 7.
2 Keener, *Miracles*, 1:371–75.

remove abusive practices and issues, primarily related to relics, Catholic apologetics, and thousands of miracle claims just before the Reformation.[3]

Much of the proposed healing ministry of the Roman Catholic Church had evolved and centered on worship of saints and relics. Impure motives and greed played a significant role in corrupting the sacraments and practice of the church. De Arteaga states how "The Church in the New Testament was persecuted and politically powerless, but filled with the miracle working power of the Spirit, and its congregations often practiced the gifts of the Spirit. The Church of the year 1500 persecuted dissent and any form of 'irregular ideas' with torture and execution, exercised great political power, but was largely empty of the gifts, presence and power of the Spirit." [4] The church had become a place filled with corrupt leaders and devoid of Christians practicing the gifts of the Spirit in a true New Testament hermeneutic modality, which included healing and deliverance.

Additionally, Luther, Calvin, and other Reformers predominately saw sickness as God's will, a result of Adamic sin, and therefore an avenue for God to bring punishment upon individuals for sin and to teach them to rely upon God during their suffering. According to Porterfield, they believed "God's will lay behind every single disease and misfortune and every particular instance of healing and prosperity. Christians should pray not to force God's hand but to align themselves with his will."[5] Despite this belief, Keener says of Luther, "On one hand, he regarded sickness and suffering as normal and a means of grace. On the other, he notes miraculous healings of himself, his wife, and Melanchthon

---

3 Keener, *Miracles*, 1:374.

4 De Arteaga, *Forging*, 75.

5 Porterfield, *Healing*, 98.

in answer to prayer; Melanchthon returned from apparent death following Luther's own prayer."[6] According to Porterfield, Calvin viewed suffering as "medicine administered by God." [7] Clark explains how Augustine's theology steered the Reformers from a "Warfare Worldview" to a "Blueprint Worldview."[8] Clark continues, "Christians began to see all things as foreordained and to passively accept what they believed to be God's will. Ultimately, this would have a very negative impact upon the theology of healing in the church."[9]

Calvin, even more so than Luther, opposed the operative graces of healing, deliverance, and miracles in the church, as they were no longer needed once true doctrine was established. Keener states, "Whereas postbiblical miracles might be disallowed, Calvinists allowed for special providence as well as general providence, the former potentially accommodating miracles under another title."[10] Porterfield says, "But healing and interpretation were in a different category entirely. They were extraordinary gifts of the spirit bestowed on Christ's earliest followers to reflect the momentous events of his actual appearance on earth, not ongoing practices of Christian life."[11] Historian Carlos Eire further states Calvin's view of miracles: "To expect miracles of healing as part of Christian faith would be to seek God in creation, and that, for Calvin, was the essence of idolatry."[12]

---

6 Keener, *Miracles*, 1:373.

7 Porterfield, *Healing*, 99.

8 Clark, *There Is More*, 69.

9 Ibid.

10 Keener, *Miracles*, 1:377. Cf. Keener footnote for additional discussion and Ruthven, *What's Wrong*, 5.

11 Porterfield, *Healing*, 95.

12 Carlos Eire, *War against the Idols: The Reformation of Worship from Erasmus to Calvin* (New York: Cambridge University Press, 1986), 224.

According to Kelsey, "Calvin was even more explicit when he came to discuss unction. There was simply no way it could be a sacrament of any miraculous power such as healing. These gifts, he said, were only temporary to begin with, because they were needed to make the preaching of the gospel wonderful."[13] Calvin took the early writings of Augustine and developed core doctrinal positions on cessationism. Kelsey states, "In fact, it was John Calvin (1509–1564), the great Reformed systematic theologian and Protestant leader of Geneva, Switzerland, who converted cessationism from a debatable theory into a core doctrine."[14] De Arteaga continues this assessment, stating, "Calvin early on adopted Augustine's cessationism, and rejected his later corrections. Why this is so is unclear. Certainly his disdain for Catholic abuses in the healing ministry was a factor. But another factor may have been his enchantment with Platonic philosophy, which disdained the body as an entrapment to the spirit."[15] Kelsey writes, "Luther clearly believed that the great miracles like healing were given in the beginning simply so that church people could later do 'greater works than these' by teaching, converting, and saving people spiritually."[16] Ruthven adds, "For what became 'mainstream' Protestantism, miracles and prophecies had only one (completed) function, that is, *to establish true doctrine.*"[17] The emphasis of the gospel of the kingdom, as demonstrated in the power of the Spirit by Christ and the early church, had clearly been removed from the Reformers' theology during the Reformation period.

While Calvin never seemed to change his staunch views against healing and the miraculous, he ironically claims to have

---

13 Kelsey, *Healing and Christianity*, 174.
14 Ibid.
15 De Arteaga, *Forging*, 81.
16 Kelsey, *Healing and Christianity*, 173.
17 Ruthven, *What's Wrong*, 5.

been healed when stricken with fever.[18] Keener states of Calvin, "Believing that apostolic miracles had ceased did not make him doubt that God could still answer prayer for healing."[19] Luther, on the other hand, like Augustine, changed or at least expressed greater openness to prayer for the sick, especially in his later years. As previously mentioned, Luther taught on prayer for the sick from Jas 5:14–15 the year before he died.[20] Luther viewed miracles as once necessary to validate the emerging church; however, he viewed most miracles performed by monks as contradicting scripture.[21] He did acknowledge that God would still perform miracles as required and that any Christian could be used to work miracles, but this was not normative any longer.[22]

According to Gordon, "If we turn from Luther the controversialist to Luther the pastor, we find a man who believed and spoke with all the vehemence of his Saxon heart on the side of present miracles."[23] Gordon states that Luther proclaimed the healing power of the name of Christ: "How often has it happened and still does, that devils have been driven out in the name of Christ, also by calling on his name and prayer that the sick have been healed?"[24] One specific account of Luther delivering a young woman from demonic oppression is telling. The young woman was brought to Luther, and he required her to recite the Apostles' Creed; however, when she came to the words "in Jesus Christ" she began to mani-

---

18 Porterfield, *Healing*, 97–98. Porterfield states of Calvin he "venerated Mary and believed that the prayers to St. Genevieve had saved his life when he was stricken with fever."

19 Keener, *Miracles*, 1:373.

20 Ibid.

21 Ibid., 1:372.

22 Ibid., 1:372–73. See Keener's footnote, "in extraordinary times, 'without exception each Christian would have the power to perform miracles.'"

23 Gordon, "Ministry of Healing," 177.

24 Ibid.

fest a demon. The next day she was brought to the church, and after Luther gave the sermon, she fell prostrate to the ground, and once again the demon manifested through kicking and screaming. Luther laid his hand on the girl's head, and repeated the Apostles' Creed, the Lord's Prayer, and also Jn 14:12. He then prayed with other ministers of the church in the name of Christ for the girl to be delivered of the demon. With his foot, he touched the girl and declared to the demon that he would not engage in a show, but rather that Satan was defeated, his head crushed and under the feet of Jesus Christ. She was taken away to her home and friends, never to be troubled again by demonic torment.[25]

On another occasion, Luther's friend and colleague at Wittenberg, Philip Melanchthon, was near death, but after Luther earnestly called upon God and prayed for him, Melanchthon dramatically recovered and was healed. Gordon describes the healing:

After this, taking the hand of Philip, and well knowing what was the anxiety of his heart and conscience, he said, "Be of good courage, Philip, thou shalt not die. Though God wanted not good reason to slay thee, yet he willeth not the death of a sinner, but that he may be converted and live. Wherefore, give not place to the spirit of grief, nor become the slayer of thyself, but trust in the Lord who is able to kill and to make alive." While he uttered these things Philip began, as it were, to revive and to breathe, and gradually recovering his strength, is at last restored to health. If the reader should conclude hastily that this recovery may be accounted for on entirely natural principles, we have to remind him that the conviction of both parties to the transaction was quite otherwise. Melanchthon writing to a friend

---

25 Thomas Boys, *The Suppressed Evidence, or Proofs of the Miraculous Faith and Experience of the Church of Christ in All Ages* (London: Hamilton, Adams and Co., 1832), 162–163.

says: "I should have been a dead man had I not been re-
called from death itself by the coming of Luther." Luther
speaks in the same manner writing to friends: "Philip is
very well after such an illness, for it was greater than I had
supposed. I found him dead, but, by an evident miracle of
God, he lives." [26]

In 1545, about five years after Melanchthon was healed and a year
before Luther himself died, Luther gave instructions for a healing service based on Jas 5:14–15. It seems Luther clearly came to
value the grace and ministry of healing. Keener states, "A year before he died, Luther taught on prayer for the sick, both privately
and in churches, following Jas 5:14–15. In a letter he noted 'prayer
for healing by the laying on of hands' occurring in Wittenberg."[27]
According to Kelsey, "The year before he died, when asked what
to do for a man who was mentally ill, Luther wrote instructions
for a healing service based on the New Testament letter of James,
adding, 'This is what we do, and that we have been accustomed to
do, for a cabinetmaker here was similarly afflicted with madness
and we cured him by prayer in Christ's name.' Like the two great
saints of the church before him, Augustine and Aquinas, he seems
to have learned in his mellower years to value, rather than to dis-
regard, this gift from God."[28] One could deduce that if this model
of ministry was good for a key Reformer, who at times opposed
the ministry of healing, one could also find the relevance of this
model for today. [29]

Other accounts of healing and deliverance are recorded during the Reformation. Kelsey describes how St. Philip Neri, St.

---

26 Gordon, "Ministry of Healing," 178–179.

27 Keener, *Miracles*, 1:373.

28 Kelsey, *Healing and Christianity*, 183.

29 Keener, *Miracles*, 1:372–373.

Francis de Sales, and others were renowned for healing the sick through prayer, touch, and the sign of the cross.[30] According to Kelsey, George Fox, founder of the Quakers in the seventeenth century, operated in the power of God, recording many of the facts in his *Journal* and in an unpublished manuscript, *Book of Miracles.*[31] According to Eddie L. Hyatt, minister and professor of theology, and author of *2000 Years of Charismatic Christianity*, on one occasion, Fox prayed for an eleven-year-old boy who was still in a cradle, having never walked. Three years later, Fox returned to this home only to be met with enthusiastic reception and joy. He learned that after he had prayed for the boy, the parents returned home only to discover the boy completely well and outside playing—it was a miracle.[32] Keener adds that "Anabaptists, Quakers, and Pietists all claimed healings. English Baptists cited a dramatic deathbed recovery from this period."[33]

The Moravians, also known as the United Brethren, who trace their spiritual roots to John Huss, a fifteenth-century reformer and martyr, affirm the continuation of healings and miracles. Gordon recounts the Moravian position regarding healing and miracles:

> We are, indeed, well aware that, so far from its being possible to prove by scripture, or by experience, that visions and dreams, the gifts of miracles, healings and other extraordinary gifts, have absolutely ceased in Christendom since the apostolic times, it is on the contrary proved, both by facts and by scripture, that there may always be these gifts where there is faith, and that they will never be entirely detached

---

30 Kelsey, *Healing and Christianity*, 183.

31 Ibid.

32 Eddie L. Hyatt, *2000 Years of Charismatic Christianity: A 21st Century Look at Church History from a Pentecostal/Charismatic Perspective* (Lake Mary, FL: Charisma House, 2002), 92.

33 Keener, *Miracles*, 1:380.

from it. We need only take care to discern the true from the false, and to distinguish from miracles proceeding from the Holy Ghost, lying miracles, or those which without being so decidedly of the devil do not so decidedly indicate the presence of the Lord.[34]

Keener states that "Eighteenth-century Moravians also reported miraculous healings; instantaneous miracle cures are especially reported in 1731, several years into the famous revival at Herrnhut."[35] Gordon cites of Moravian leader and revivalist Nikolaus von Zinzendorf that he attested to healings and miracles in the movement, including those healed of cancer: "To believe against hope is the root of the gift of miracles; and I owe this testimony to our beloved Church, that apostolic powers are there manifested. We have had undeniable proofs thereof in the unequivocal discovery of things, persons, and circumstances, which could not humanly have been discovered, in the healing of maladies in themselves incurable, such as cancers, consumptions, when the patient was in the agonies of death, etc., all by means of prayer, or of a single word."[36]

Writing about the First Great Awakening in the American colonies, Keener writes, "Although earlier Reformed thinkers, including Puritans, had largely embraced forms of cessationism, some ideas began to shift during the later phase of the Great Awakening."[37] Supernatural activity was part of the Awakening, and some evangelical leaders emphasized the activity of the Spirit, and some even allowed for physical healings.[38] One of the key lead-

34 Gordon, 160.
35 Keener, *Miracles*, 1:380.
36 Gordon, "Ministry of Healing," 161.
37 Keener, *Miracles*, 1:381.
38 Keener, *Miracles*, 1:381

ers of the Awakening, Jonathan Edwards, noted that both physical and mental health accompanied the revival, observing a decline in sickness and depression.[39]

John Wesley, eighteenth-century Anglican theologian and founder of Methodism, believed in healing and the miraculous work of the Spirit, having himself received healing more than once. Keener states of Wesley, "John Wesley, who unlike some theologians of his era, spent more time on the front lines of evangelism than in academic circles, challenged some cessationist views of his contemporaries."[40] Wesley was once overcome by a fever and cough; he asked God to increase his faith and to confirm his promise of healing: "These signs shall follow them that believe" (Mk 16:17). While still praying, his pain vanished and the fever left him. In Wesley's words,

> I was obliged to lie down most of the day, being easy only in that posture. In the evening, beside the pain in my back and head, and the fever which still continued upon me, just as I began to pray I was seized with such a cough that I could hardly speak. At the same time came strongly to my mind, "These signs shall follow them that believe." I called aloud on Jesus to increase my faith and to confirm the word of His grace. While I was speaking, my pain vanished away, the fever left me, my bodily strength returned and for many weeks I felt neither weakness nor pain. Unto thee, O Lord, do I give thanks.[41]

---

39 Ibid.

40 Ibid., 1:383.

41 John Wesley, *The Works of John Wesley*, Vol. 8 (Grand Rapids: MI, Zondervan Publishing House, 1958), 458–459.

According to Kelsey, "John Wesley described numerous miracles of God's healing, many of them through his own prayers."[42] When asked once about individuals under his ministry receiving miraculous healings, Wesley responded by stating his conviction that the healings were not merely natural, but a consequence of prayer and the supernatural power of God: "As it can be proved by abundance of witnesses that these cures were frequently (indeed almost always) the instantaneous consequences of prayer, your inference is just. I cannot, dare not, affirm that they were purely natural. I believe they were not. I believe many of them were wrought by the supernatural power of God."[43] Keener recounts of Wesley: "Wesley's brother Charles was raised from a debilitating attack of pleurisy and apparently unconsciousness when a woman moved by a dream declared, 'In the name of Jesus Christ of Nazareth arise and believe, and thou shalt be healed of all thy infirmities.'"[44] Wesley was not the only Methodist minister to cite healings; John Valton also claimed healings and even rainfall in meetings as a result of prayer.[45] Wesley expected normal signs of the Holy Spirit in his meetings.[46]

Wesley stated clearly his belief in the continuation of miraculous gifts throughout the church age: "I do not recollect any Scripture wherein we are taught that miracles were to be confined within the limits either of the apostolic age or the Cyprian age, or of any period of time, longer or shorter, even till the restitution of all things."[47]

---

42 Kelsey, *Healing and Christianity*, 184. Cf. Keener, *Miracles*, 1:383.

43 Wesley, *Works*, 8:457.

44 Keener, *Miracles*, 1:383.

45 Ibid.

46 Ibid., 1:383–84.

47 Wesley, *Works*, 8:465.

Chapter 11

HEALING AND DELIVERANCE, AD 1750–PRESENT

Despite the negative influence of cessationism and Enlightenment thinking during the seventeenth through nineteenth centuries, new movements began to emerge in the church by the late nineteenth century, both Catholic and Protestant, which embraced the New Testament ministry model of healing and deliverance. Kelsey describes a renewed interest in healing during this period: "In the late years of the nineteenth century a new interest in religious healing began to take place in Europe and America. It bypassed most of the established churches, but has touched a great many people all over the world."[1] Keener adds, "By the late nineteenth century, a much broader and more consistent healing movement than among earlier US Protestants grew from the circles that were heavily emphasizing holiness."[2] Many argued that one of the emphases of this new healing movement was that

---

1 Kelsey, *Healing and Christianity*, 185.
2 Keener, *Miracles*, 1:390.

healing was in the atonement and therefore, like salvation from sin, was available to all.[3]

The Roman Catholic Church has documented extensively more than fourteen hundred miracles during the past four centuries.[4] In Lourdes, France, beginning in 1885, numerous healings and miracles began to be reported.[5] Although many of the French Catholic leaders were initially hesitant about miracle claims at Lourdes, unlike many of the Reformers and key leaders in Protestantism, Catholics had not embraced cessationism and therefore were more receptive to reports of healing and miracles. According to Keener, there were "a number of prominent nineteenth-century Protestants, like A. B. Simpson, who affirmed the genuineness and divine character of such Catholic miracles while demurring from Catholic theology."[6] A. B. Simpson (1843-1919) was a Canadian preacher, theologian, author, and founder of the Christian and Missionary Alliance church, a Protestant church which had an emphasis on world evangelism.

Almost simultaneously in the late nineteenth century, within Protestant ranks, a new awareness of present-day healing ministry began to emerge on a global scale. De Arteaga writes, "All through the Nineteenth Century the Holy Spirit moved in powerful revivals, challenging the doctrine of cessationism at the very time it was reaching peak influence. Revivals broke out in England, South Africa, India and the United States, and brought with them different gifts of the Holy Spirit for all to see."[7]

Nineteenth-century German pastor Johann Christoph Blumhardt had a healing ministry that began in 1842, with the

---

3 Keener, *Miracles*, 1:390.

4 Ibid., 1:384.

5 Ibid., 1:385.

6 Keener, *Miracles*, 1:385–86.

7 De Arteaga, *Forging*, 181.

healing of a girl in his church who was seriously disturbed, accompanied by unexplained psychic phenomena.[8] Kelsey writes of this healing, "Blumhardt himself found the power of the Spirit through this confrontation, and both he and his parish were changed by it."[9] Keener writes, "Blumhardt viewed healings as foreshadowings of the kingdom, and initially hoped that the cures experienced in his ministry might be signs that the expected eschatological outpouring of the Spirit and renewal of gifts was at hand."[10] Rudolf Bultmann rejected the miracle claims of Blumhardt; however, Karl Barth named Blumhardt as one of three people who were among his mentors, and Jürgen Moltmann noted Blumhardt's influence on his own "theology of hope."[11] Considering the influence of theologians Bultmann, Barth, and Moltmann, the healing ministry of Blumhardt is significant and provides further evidence of the importance of a discipleship hermeneutic that includes the *charisms* of the Spirit.

Regarding influential US leaders in the healing movement of the time, Dr. Charles Cullis and Presbyterian minister William Boardman in 1873 went to Europe to learn from the models of Trudel and Blumhardt.[12] De Arteaga says of Cullis, "The father of the Faith-Cure movement was Dr. Charles Cullis (1833–1892), a homeopathic physician from Boston. Though not the first to be involved in a full-time healing ministry, he had the administrative ability and commanded the professional respect to bring Christian

---

8 Kelsey, *Healing and Christianity*, 185.

9 Ibid.

10 Keener, *Miracles*, 1:389.

11 Ibid.; cf. Kelsey, *Healing and Christianity*, 185. According to Keener and Kelsey, Barth criticized Bultmann for his rejection of the miracle claims of Blumhardt. Kelsey writes, "Barth accepted Blumhardt's idea that a struggle with the devil offered 'new light' on healing in the New Testament."

12 Ibid., 1:391.

healing to national attention."[13] Regarding *Faith Cures*, which Cullis wrote in 1879, De Arteaga states, "*Faith Cures* contained a brief commentary on the major healing Scripture verses from the Old and New Testaments, a description of how he entered the healing ministry and a series of testimonial letters of the healing of patients at his refuges. Significantly, Dr. Cullis stated clearly that there was no conflict between faith healing and medical practice and that he constantly used both in his ministry. This balanced and mature theological view was unusual for its time."[14]

Arising from the earlier seventeenth- and eighteenth-century Pietist and Puritan movements, the nineteenth-century Wesleyan holiness revival emerged. According to De Arteaga, "This was the Holiness revival itself, a theological reenergizing of John Wesley's theology, followed by the first great Christian healing revival since New Testament times, the Faith-Cure Movement."[15] De Arteaga describes this healing revival as follows:

> The first *sustained focused and self-conscious* healing revival of modern Christendom occurred in the latter years of the 19th Century among American evangelicals who were part of, or influenced by, the Holiness and Perfectionist movements. It had various names such as the Divine Healing Movement, or the Evangelical Healing Movement, but it was known at the time principally as the Faith-Cure movement. In this revival, healing was not merely an unexpected by-product of fervent prayer but the result of intended and directed prayer efforts.[16]

---

13 De Arteaga, *Forging*, 187.
14 Ibid., 189–190.
15 Ibid., 102.
16 Ibid., 187.

According to Heather D. Curtis, an associate professor of Religion at Tufts University, in 1885 prominent leaders of this nineteenth-century divine healing movement gathered from around the globe in London to take part in a service of anointing for divine healing.[17] Curtis continues, "After explaining the biblical basis for the practices of anointing, laying on of hands, and prayer for healing in passages such as James 5, the session's chair, the Reverend William E. Boardman beseeched his audience to entrust their bodies and souls to 'the Lord Jesus Christ, the *real healer.*'"[18] Curtis states that leaders such as Simpson and Elizabeth Baxter were in attendance, and that "according to these interpreters, healing had always been a part of the Christian tradition, but many believers had 'lost faith in Christ as healer.'"[19]

Keener writes of some of the early leaders of this movement, "Baptist minister A. J. Gordon, for whom Gordon College and Gordon Conwell Theological Seminary are named, A. B. Simpson, founder of Christian Missionary Alliance, Presbyterian William Boardman, and others became widely accepted figures in [the] late nineteenth- and early twentieth-century healing movement."[20] Simpson, a former Presbyterian minister who once held to cessationist views of healings and miracles, personally received divine healing while attending meetings with Cullis in 1881.[21] According to Curtis, Simpson, after studying the scriptures, deduced that "the atonement of Christ takes away sin and the consequence of sin for every believer who accepts him"; therefore, healing "was

---

17 Heather D. Curtis, "The Global Character of Nineteenth-Century Divine Healing," in *Global Pentecostal and Charismatic Healing*, ed. Candy Gunther Brown (New York: Oxford University Press, 2011), 29.

18 Ibid., 29.

19 Curtis, "Global Character," 31.

20 Keener, *Miracles*, 1:393–94.

21 Curtis, "Global Character," 35.

included in the gospel of Jesus Christ, as purchased and finished for all who accepted Jesus fully."[22] Porterfield states, "American revivalist Maria Woodworth Etter (1844–1924) and other charismatic preachers incorporated healing into their religious meetings in the Midwest."[23] Curtis describes the global spread of divine healing during this period: "By 1885, divine healing had spread from Switzerland and Germany across Europe and to Great Britain, the United States, Australia, and India."[24]

By the twentieth century, Pentecostalism, with its emphasis on *glossolalia* and healing, was emerging primarily from the Holiness branch within the Methodist church, evangelical revivalism, and from participants of the Keswick "Higher Life" and "Faith-Cure" movements.[25] De Arteaga writes of this period, "Finally, these streams fed into the Pentecostal revival made famous in the Asuza Street revival of 1906 where the gifts of the Spirit were fully recovered and made central. But again, the Pharisaic and Sadduccaic heretics within the churches attacked, marginalized and limited both the Faith-Cure movement and Pentecostalism."[26] Keener states, "Apart from its addition of speaking in tongues, Pentecostalism essentially continued the ideals of the healing movement that had already been circulating at the turn of the century."[27] Henry I. Lederle, professor of Theology and Missions at Sterling College, writes, "Pentecostals view their historical roots as stretching back to the first century, but it is undeniable that the foundations of the modern Pentecostal movement (like those of

---

22 Curtis, "Global Character," 31.

23 Porterfield, *Healing*, 168.

24 Curtis, "Global Character," 33.

25 Porterfield, *Healing*, 168. Cf. Vinson Synan, *The Century of the Holy Spirit: 100 Years of Pentecostal and Charismatic Renewal* (Nashville, TN: Thomas Nelson, 2001), 29–32.

26 De Arteaga, *Forging*, 102.

27 Keener, *Miracles*, 1:413–14

the ecumenical movement) are established in the eighteenth and nineteenth centuries."[28]

In general, the faith healing movement of the late nineteenth century was respected within Protestantism.[29] However, tensions and differences in theological beliefs and practices began to emerge within the healing movement. Keener continues, "In reaction against the less culturally respected early twentieth century Pentecostal movement, even Simpson's Christian Alliance distanced itself from its own doctrine of healing in the atonement."[30] Gordon emphasized that the atonement of Christ did provide for bodily healing; however, not all should be expected to be healed immediately.[31] D. L. Moody, nineteenth-century American evangelist and publisher, who also founded the Moody Bible Institute, affirmed that God could heal today, but denied that healing was in the atonement, and felt that such views were extreme.[32]

In addition to theological differences, societal worldviews affected the rise of Pentecostalism at the beginning of the twentieth century. Lederle states, "Yet the rise of Pentecostalism challenged the dominant worldview held in the West at the beginning of the twentieth century. Only in this context may we grasp the intensity of societal reaction against Azusa Street revival and its full-scale rejection."[33] Lederle continues, "Modern Christianity caricatured Pentecostalism abusively because Pentecostalism shook the very

---

28 Henry I. Lederle, *Theology with Spirit: The Future of the Pentecostal & Charismatic Movements in the Twenty-First Century* (Tulsa, OK: Word & Spirit Press, 2010), 8.

29 Keener, *Miracles*, 1:395.

30 Ibid., 1:395–96. Keener writes, "John Alexander Dowie was more radical than most contemporaries, opposing doctors and medicine and insisting on healing only through faith. While many cures are reported under Dowie's ministry, some of those who refused medical treatment died."

31 Ibid., 1:396.

32 Ibid.

33 Lederle, *Theology with Spirit*, 17.

foundations of modernism—the pervasive paradigm and framework that Christian modernism had struggled to develop over
several centuries as it accommodated itself to the secular scien-
tific rationalism of the day."[34] Curtis states, "Despite several rifts,
however, divine healing remained a remarkably vibrant movement
whose members envisioned themselves as participants in a global
revitalization and expansion of Christianity."[35]

With the outpouring of the Holy Spirit in Wales in 1904 and
then at Azusa Street in 1906, the modern Pentecostal movement
was well underway. Vinson Synan, historian, author and Dean of
the School of Divinity at Regent University, describes the hunger for the Holy Spirit at the turn of the twentieth century: "Just
as the holiness movement set the stage for the birth of modern
Pentecostalism, so the Welsh Revival of 1904 clearly demonstrated
the world-wide hunger for such a renewal."[36] Curtis states, "In the
early decades of the twentieth century, the outbreak of Pentecostal
revivals all over the globe fulfilled, for many proponents of divine
healing, the fervent hope that 'the fullness of Pentecost' had finally come."[37] Pentecostalism spread globally from the Azusa Street
revival, with numerous healings and miracles cited both during
and after this outpouring of the Holy Spirit. Keener lists several significant healings that took place during the Azusa revival,
and by his own admission of the numbers of healings, he said,
"One can barely enumerate the stories."[38] De Arteaga states of the
Azusa Street revival, "The initial revival at Azusa Street lasted between 1906–1909, with another burst occurring after 1911. Besides

---

34 Lederle, *Theology with Spirit*, 43.

35 Curtis, "Global Character," 43.

36 Synan, *Century of the Holy Spirit*, 41.

37 Curtis, "Global Character," 43.

38 Keener, *Miracles*, 1:415–16. Cf. 415–19 for more Azusa testimonies and global
Pentecostal accounts of healing during this era.

bringing thousands of skeptics and non-believers to the Lord, many thousands were baptized in the Spirit, and many healed."[39]

An important dimension to Pentecostalism and early Pentecostal leaders was the message and ministry of divine healing. According to Keener, "nearly all early Pentecostal leaders claimed 'stunning divine healings in their own bodies.'"[40] Several prominent healing ministers of the early twentieth century claimed thousands of healings and miracles—for example, John G. Lake, in Africa and also in North America, Charles S. Price, Maria Woodworth-Etter, Smith Wigglesworth, F. F. Bosworth, and Aimee Semple McPherson.[41] By the middle of the twentieth century, other healing evangelists and ministers were continuing the theme of divine healing as normative Christian practice. Perhaps most well known, Oral Roberts, healing evangelist and founder of Oral Roberts University, came to the forefront during the healing revivals of the late 1940s and 1950s.[42] Despite criticism that has occurred against the healing movement and healing evangelists of the late twentieth century, this ministry of healing has continued with effectiveness in modern Christianity. Keener and Brown have gone to great lengths to discuss and document current trends and miracle claims in both the twentieth and twenty-first centuries.[43]

---

39 De Arteaga, *Forging*, 215.
40 Keener, *Miracles*, 1:419.
41 Ibid., 1:419–24.
42 Ibid., 1:424.
43 Cf. Keener, *Miracles*, vols. 1 and 2, and Brown, *Global*.

Section 3

THEOLOGICAL
CONSIDERATIONS

Chapter 12

THEOLOGICAL OVERVIEW

The purpose of this section is to examine the theology that supports the ministry of healing and deliverance in the church. As demonstrated in the historical section, church history records a theology that supports the belief and practice of the *charisms* of the Spirit, including healing and deliverance. In this section, Christology, pneumatology, and soteriology will be examined to support the theological foundations of healing and deliverance ministry for today.

As previously discussed in the historical section, church history reveals that healing and deliverance ministry has been an integral part of the culture and growth of the church since Christ and the early disciples. Despite a diminished influence of this ministry during the Middle Ages, the Reformation, and the Enlightenment, there has been a renewed emphasis upon healing and deliverance ministry since the nineteenth century. Irrespective of theological changes toward healing and deliverance ministry during previous eras of the church, these graces have continued throughout the history of the church and into our postmodern era.

As discussed in the biblical section, in looking at the life and ministry of Jesus, even the most casual reader of the Gospels should conclude that Jesus spent his time teaching about the kingdom of God, healing the sick, casting out demons, and performing miracles as routine. He then replicated this ministry by giving his disciples authority and power over sickness, disease, and demonic powers and instructing them to continue his ministry model. Jesus instructed and sent the original apostles and disciples to teach others what they were taught and commanded previously (cf. Mt 10:7–8; Lk 10:1; Mt 28:18–20). According to De Arteaga,

> Further, we can assume that the seventy-two disciples sent out at the beginning of Jesus' ministry (Lk 10) were at various levels of spiritual development. Some had sought God earnestly for a long time, and others just awakened and [were] immature. Regardless of their level of spiritual maturity, they all shared the *disciples' authority* to do the miraculous healings/exorcisms that made proclamation of the Kingdom effective. This is an important issue. In future centuries this disciples' authority would be blighted by the assumption that only those of advanced spiritual attainment, such as monks or other saintly persons, could minister healing or deliverance.[1]

The disciples were taught how to heal the sick, cast out demons, and proclaim the gospel of the kingdom, not just in word but in power (1 Cor 4:20).[2] This was normative Christian ministry and theology for the early church, and Christ intended it to be common theology and ministry practice for all who would believe and

---

1 De Arteaga, *Forging*, 10.

2 Cf. Ruthven, DMin Cohort Notes, 16. "*The kingdom of God does not consist in talk but in power* (*dunamis* = miracle power). Note: Kingdom of God *defined as dunamis* = healing, exorcism, signs and wonders. Also includes repentance and power over sin."

follow him until his *Parousia*. The *charism* of healing was to be an integral part of the gospel proclamation, and Jesus deliberately taught his disciples in this kingdom ministry model with the understanding that they would be his successors, teaching and training others to do the same. [3] Keener states, "Perhaps Jesus even deliberately trained his disciples as his successors, as teachers normally trained their disciples to be, expecting them to be able to perform the same activity that he did (cf. Mk 9:18–19, 28–29; 11:23; Lk 9:40–41; 17:6)."[4] According to Kelsey, "It is also clear that Jesus sent his disciples out to continue this basic ministry (Mk 6:7–13; Mt 10:5–10; Lk 9:1–6). The book of Acts records how well they carried out this commission. It is difficult to see how Bultmann, and many who follow him, can eliminate this entire ministry on theological and philosophical grounds by calling it mythology."[5]

An important theological question to ask today is, "Through normal Christians, does God still heal the sick, cast out demons, and perform miracles as in the days of the earthly ministry of Christ and his early followers?" If the answer is yes, as the tenor of New Testament scripture alludes to, historical data points to, and many theological views adhere to, then it behooves the church to learn, believe, and practice this ministry of Christ and of his church. Within the study of Christology, pneumatology, and soteriology, the link between Christ's kingdom mission and ministry, in both word and power, is at present demonstrated and evidenced through his church and through individuals by the power of the Holy Spirit.

---

3 Borobio, "Enquiry into Healing," 38.

4 Keener, *Miracles*, 1:29.

5 Kelsey, *Healing and Christianity*, 43.

Chapter 13

CHRISTOLOGY AND PNEUMATOLOGY

The doctrine of Christ or Christology is the basis and foundation for our understanding of theology.[1] As Karl Barth, regarded by many as one of the greatest theologians of the twentieth century, stated succinctly, "Dogmatics must actually be Christology and only Christology."[2] The essence of all Christian theology is rooted in the being, nature, and function of Christ. As Owen C. Thomas, former professor of Theology at Episcopal Divinity School and current adjunct faculty member at the Graduate Theological Union, and Ellen K. Wondra, professor of Theology and Ethics at Seabury-Western Theological Seminary, state in *Introduction to Theology*, "Christology is not a matter of attempting to reconcile the incarnation with a doctrine of God that we have already...; it is the basis of the Christian doctrine of God."[3]

---

1 Owen C. Thomas and Ellen K. Wondra, *Introduction to Theology* (Harrisburg, PA: Morehouse Publishing, 2002), 158.

2 Ibid.

3 Ibid.

When studying Christology, it is important to consider both the work (function) of Christ and the being (nature) of Christ; these two aspects are inseparable. As Paul Tillich, who like Barth, is regarded as one of the most influential theologians of the twentieth century, stated in his *Systematic Theology*, "The being of Christ is his work, and his work is his being."[4] According to Clark H. Pinnock, who was professor emeritus of Systematic Theology at McMaster Divinity College, in his *Flame of Love: A Theology of the Holy Spirit*, "Anointing by the Spirit is central for understanding the person and work of Jesus—more central than theology has normally made it. Christology must not lack for pneumatology."[5] To understand Christ's being, we must also understand Christ's work, and his work can only effectively be understood in terms of the anointing by the Holy Spirit, as Jesus stated in Lk 4:18 (NRSV): "The Spirit of the Lord is upon me, because he has anointed me." According to James D. G. Dunn, New Testament scholar and professor emeritus of Theology at University of Durham,

> We may note particularly Mt 12.28/Lk 11.20—"Since it is by the Spirit (or finger) of God that I cast out demons, then has come upon you the kingdom of God"—where the order of the words draws the hearers' attention to the Spirit (finger) of God as the source of the power which made his act (or word) of exorcism so effective. This was evidently Jesus' own explanation for his success as a healer—and it is in terms of an empowering by the Spirit (or agency) of God. Similarly there is clear enough evidence that Jesus thought of himself as one in whom Is 61 was being fulfilled: the Spirit of the Lord was upon him, because the Lord had

---

4 Paul Tillich, *Systematic Theology* (Chicago: University of Chicago Press, 1951), 2:168.

5 Clark H. Pinnock, *Flame of Love: A Theology of the Holy Spirit* (Downers Grove, IL: Inter Varsity Press Academic, 1996), 79.

anointed him to bring good tidings to the poor...(note particularly Lk 6.20f/Mt 5.3–6; Mt 11.5/Lk 7.22). [6]

It is for these reasons Christology and pneumatology, or the study of Christ and the study of the Holy Spirit, will be discussed within this same section, developing an understanding of Spirit Christology.

The Nicene Creed declared that "Christ was of the same substance (*homoousios*) with God," thus contradicting Arian belief and affirming that Jesus was divine. The Chalcedonian definition states, "Jesus is truly divine and truly human," which further substantiates both the divinity and humanity of Christ. In defining the communication of attributes, the Patristic fathers established that Jesus is both fully divine and fully human, two natures in one *hypostasis*. The Logos, who existed from eternity, became human, his divine nature united with human flesh—the Word (*logos*) became flesh (Jn 1:14). In discussing orthodoxy and the early church creeds (which sought to make them as clear as possible without distortion), Thomas and Wondra state, "The church rejected all attempts to qualify it....Thus orthodox Christianity does not attempt to explain the substance of Christology, that is, how the two natures are united in one person. It attempts to indicate where the mystery lies, so to speak, and to defend the mystery against the attempts to dissolve it into a neat formula that would distort it." [7]

However, as Pinnock elaborates, it is important to mention that traditional orthodox theology, with its emphasis upon the divine Logos becoming flesh, tends to focus only upon the "descent of the Logos and ignore the work of the Spirit in the Son." [8] Pinnock

---

6 James D. G. Dunn, "The Spirit of Christ," in *Christology in the Making* (London: SCM Press, 1989), 135.

7 Thomas and Wondra, *Introduction to Theology*, 164.

8 Pinnock, *Flame of Love*, 80–81.

continues, "Yet it is striking how systematic theologies, in explicating the divine-human person of Christ, forget altogether about the Spirit. It was the anointing by the Spirit that made Jesus 'Christ,' not the hypostatic union, and it was the anointing that made him effective in history as the absolute Savior. Jesus was ontologically Son of God from the moment of conception, but he became Christ by the power of the Spirit."[9] Pinnock continues with this concept: "Logos Christology is ontologically focused, while a Spirit Christology is functionally focused, but the two work together."[10] Oscar Cullman, a twentieth-century Christian theologian in the Lutheran tradition, also advocates a functional Christology, instead of the ontologically based Christology that emerged in the Patristic era, he states in *The Christology of the New Testament*: "[I]n the light of the New Testament witness, all mere speculation about [Christ's] nature is an absurdity. Functional Christology is the only kind which exists."[11]

The person of Christ, fully human and yet fully divine, was able to suffer, endure temptation, laugh, cry, and so forth. His divine being was united to his human flesh, possessing a rational soul. He had a human nature, he had a will, and he had feelings and emotions. According to Alister E. McGrath, professor of Theology and Religion at the University of Oxford, Luther's application of the communication of attributes led to his "crucified God theology" that "Jesus Christ suffered and died. Jesus Christ is God. Therefore God suffered and died."[12] In other words, Luther counters Patristic theology (which was heavily influenced by Greek philosophy) that

---

9 Pinnock, *Flame of Love*, 80–81.

10 Ibid., 91.

11 Oscar Cullman, *The Christology of the New Testament* (Philadelphia, PA: Westminster Press, 1959), 8.

12 Alister E. McGrath, *Christian Theology: An Introduction* (Chichester, UK: Wiley-Blackwell, 2011), 281.

adhered to the impassibility of God. [13] Luther's theological view is important as it relates to redemption and healing as God in Christ suffered for us, yet the humanity of Christ took our place on the cross. Through his humanity, our sins, our sorrows, and our sickness, disease, and pain were atoned for, and the provision for healing of the whole person was made available (cf. Is 53:4-5; 1 Pt 2:24).

Our salvation, acquired through the redemption of Christ, encompasses every aspect of our being and nature. We are saved (*sozo*) spirit, soul, and body—all of our emotions, feelings, pains, ailments, disease, and sin are being redeemed in Christ. Since Christ has fully assumed a human nature (not just a human body), our redemption is therefore complete and comprehensive of our entire being. Further, as will be examined more closely in the chapter on soteriology, our redemption (salvation) is not merely eschatological but is available now and involves healing and deliverance for our spirit, soul, and body presently.

Irenaeus and Athanasius stated a key theological point regarding both Christ and humanity's relationship to God's divine nature: "God became human, in order that humans might become God."[14] As Peter explained in 2 Pt 1:4 (NRSV), in Christ believers "may become participants of the divine nature." Stated another

---

13 Ruthven, DMin Cohort Notes, 3–7. Ruthven states, "Second Century apologists sought to defend Christianity in the face of persecution, slander and intellectual attack—to make Christianity understandable (and acceptable) to Greco-Roman and Jewish audience—to bridge the gap between this 'barbarian' religion and the culture of the day. Theology was recast into Greek categories: 'High' view of God's transcendence: 'God is the "uncreated, eternal, invisible, impassible, incomprehensible, and infinite, who can be apprehended by mind and reason alone, who is encompassed by light, beauty, spirit, and indescribable power, and who created, adorned, and now rules the universe" (Athenagoras, *Supplication*, 10:1).'" Cf. Thomas and Wondra, *Introduction to Theology*, 165, "Most contemporary theologians would agree, however, that although the use of Hellenistic philosophy was a necessity, it was not adequate to the task of Christology."

14 McGrath, *Christian Theology*, 339. Cf. Irenaeus, *Against Heresies*, 3.19.1; Athanasius, *On the Incarnation*, 2.54.

way, because Christ is divine, yet became human, in Christ we are human and yet possess aspects of God's divine nature. Writing of Cyril of Alexandria, Patriarch of Alexandria and leading church father in the fifth century, Matthew J. Pereira, visiting professor of Theology at Loyola Marymount University, states, "Cyril contends that fellowship with the divine nature (*theosis physis*) depends on the Holy Spirit, who is necessarily consubstantial (*homoousios*) with the Father and Son."[15] Pereira continues regarding Cyril: "In the seventh Dialogue, Cyril proclaims that Christians are temples of God, who exist (*ontos*) and subsist (*huphistemi*) in virtue of their conjunction (*synapheia*) and fellowship (*koinonia*) with the divine (*theosis*) and ineffable nature (*physis*)."[16] Pereira concludes regarding Cyril: "Well situated within the pro-Nicene tradition, Cyril concludes that the divinization of humanity would be groundless if the Holy Spirit was separated from the divine nature (*physis*) and substance (*ousiodes*)."[17] For Irenaeus, Athanasius, and Cyril, partaking of the divine nature for the believer seemed to be the natural conclusion of their Trinitarian theology.

Pinnock concurs and states that God's goal in uniting himself to humanity has been achieved through Christ, and the "divinization of the world is beginning to be realized. In Christ, humanity is elevated to the life of God."[18] Pinnock continues this thought: "What we call union (theosis or divinization) is not pantheism—there is no absorption of the person in God. By the grace of God and *as creatures* we participate in him. United to Christ without becoming Christ, we are also united to God without becoming God.

---

15 Matthew J. Pereira, "The Internal Coherence of Cyril of Alexandria's Pneumatology: Interpreting the 7th Dialogue of the *Dialogues on the Trinity*," *Union Seminary Quarterly Review* 62, no. 3–4 (January 1, 2010): 72.

16 Pereira, "The Internal Coherence of Cyril," 91.

17 Ibid.

18 Pinnock, *Flame of Love*, 81.

It is a personal union in which the distinction between Creator and creature is maintained. We enter the dance of the Trinity not as equals but as adopted partners."[19]

For some, this may seem an egalitarian view of our relationship with God, when in reality we are faced with an antinomy, a paradox that is true yet untrue. We are human, yet also participate in the divine nature and new creation reality through Christ (cf. 2 Pt 1:4; 2 Cor 5:17). The new birth in Christ has changed the believer's nature; Christians now participate in God's divine nature, are filled with the Holy Spirit, and have the potential to live a Spirit-filled life that is simply not of this earthly realm or normal to those who are not redeemed. Furthermore, we have become both heirs of God and joint-heirs with Christ, according to Rom 8:17. We are at once both human and reborn in the nature of God through Christ, thereby containing the essence of God's divine nature by the indwelling of the Holy Spirit.

By God's foreknowledge and design, we were predestined in Christ to be recreated into the image of God by the indwelling life of the Holy Spirit. This indwelling and empowering is twofold. First, it empowers us to live a life exemplifying the holy nature of God as evidenced through the fruit of the Spirit in our lives. Secondly, and equally as important, it empowers us to live a life in the power of the Spirit to effectively witness, proclaim, and demonstrate the kingdom of God to an unbelieving world. Acts 1:8 declares (NRSV), "But you will receive power when the Holy Spirit has come upon you; and you will be my witnesses in Jerusalem, in all Judea and Samaria, and to the ends of the earth." Power (*dunamis*) is necessary and normal for believers to effectively witness for Christ. The indwelling and empowering by the Holy Spirit not only enables us to participate with God's divine nature, but it equips us

---

19 Pinnock, *Flame of Love*, 154.

to proclaim the message of the kingdom in power through signs and wonders.

Charles Wesley, leader and songwriter in Methodism during the eighteenth century, held a Trinitarian understanding of the relationship between the believer and the divine nature of God. In writing about the causal effect of new birth upon an individual, Wesley states, "Christ is formed in his heart by faith. He is one with Christ and Christ with him. He is a real partaker of the divine nature. Truly his fellowship is with the Father and the Son. The Father and the Son are come unto him and make their abode with him, and his very body is the temple of the Holy Ghost."[20] Jason E. Vickers, professor of Theology and Wesleyan Studies at United Theological Seminary, continues, "Indeed, when Charles speaks of the Holy Spirit enabling us to become 'partakers of the divine nature,' he has in mind nothing less than our being caught up in the 'fellowship' of God's Triune life. The indwelling of the Holy Spirit leads directly and immediately to the mutual indwelling of the Triune God in the believer and the believer in the Triune."[21] Vickers adds, "For Charles, the work of the Holy Spirit in enabling persons to become 'partakers of the divine nature' is so important that he makes the reception of the Holy Spirit and the partaking of the divine nature the criterion of Christian identity and the distinguishing mark of 'pure religion.'"[22] Vickers concludes quoting Charles Wesley: "Dost thou know what religion is? That it is a

---

20 Kenneth G. C. Newport, ed. *The Sermons of Charles Wesley: A Critical Edition and Introduction and Notes* (Oxford, UK: Oxford University Press, 2001), sermon 7, 203, quoted in Jason E. Vickers, "Charles Wesley's Doctrine of the Holy Spirit: A Vital Resource for the Renewal of Methodism Today," *Asbury Journal* 61, no. 1 (2006): 51. Cf. John 14:16–17, 23.

21 Vickers, "Charles Wesley's Doctrine," 51.

22 Ibid.

participation in the divine nature, the life of God in the soul of man; Christ in thee, the hope of glory."[23]

For Wesley, true religion and the very life of God are found in the heart of the believer by the indwelling presence of the Holy Spirit, enabling participation with the divine nature. Since we are so entwined with the Trinity and subsequently the divine nature through our faith in Christ, should we not expect the divine life to flow from our hearts in multifaceted expressions of God's grace? After all, was not this precisely what Jesus was referring to in the Gospel of John when he said that he would give us another helper, one just like himself, the Spirit of truth, who would dwell with us and be in us (cf. Jn 14:16, 17, 21, 23, 26; 15:26; 16:7, 13)?

The nature of God is best seen through Christ; Jesus is a reflection of God, and God is like Jesus. Jesus said, "Whoever has seen me has seen the Father" (Jn 14:9 NRSV). Representing both his divine and human nature, Christ healed, delivered the oppressed, performed miracles, and demonstrated the love and kingdom of God to humanity as one who was dependent upon the Holy Spirit. According to Pinnock,

> The Spirit is more central to the story of Jesus than theology has usually acknowledged. It was by the Spirit that Jesus was conceived, anointed, empowered, commissioned, directed and raised up. We emphasize God's sending the Son and must not lose the balance of a double sending. God sends both Son and Spirit. Irenaeus spoke of them as God's two hands, implying a joint mission (*Against Heresies* 4.20.1). The relationship is dialectical. The Son is sent in the power of the Spirit, and the Spirit is poured out by the risen Lord. The missions are intertwined and equal; one is not major

---

23 Newport, *Sermons of Charles Wesley*, sermon 8, 218, quoted in Vickers, "Charles Wesley's Doctrine," 58.

and the other minor. It is not right to be Christocentric if being Christocentric means subordinating the Spirit to the Son. The two are partners in the work of redemption.[24]

The link between Christology and pneumatology is evident in the New Testament and ministry practice of Christ. Arthur Michael Ramsey, twentieth-century Anglican bishop and the 100th Archbishop of Canterbury, stated, "The importance of the confession 'Jesus is Lord' is not only that Jesus is divine, but that God is Christlike,"[25] which enlarges our understanding of the divinity of Christ, the humanity of Christ, the nature of God, and the Trinitarian reality of Christology. Jesus, while being both divine and yet human, revealed the nature of God through dependence on the Spirit and gave all believers an example of how to live by the leading and empowerment of the Holy Spirit.

Greig explains that Jesus and the apostles taught their disciples to hear God's voice, depend on the Holy Spirit, and then do the works that Christ did: "Jesus called His disciples into an intimate relationship with himself ('that they might be with him' Mk 3:14), taught them the message of the kingdom orally (Mk 4:11), showed them the ministry of the kingdom in His casting out demons and healing the sick, and then sent them with his authority and power to do the same."[26] Greig continues, "The apostles not only proclaimed the Gospel with preaching and healing, but they also taught *all* the disciples they made to depend on the Holy Spirit and to proclaim the Gospel with preaching and healing."[27]

---

24 Pinnock, *Flame of Love*, 81–82.
25 McGrath, *Christian Theology*, 267.
26 Greig, "Power Evangelism," 16.
27 Ibid., 17.

In early church tradition, the writers of the New Testament saw the connection between the Spirit resting upon Christ and the power he operated in to heal and perform miracles. Acts 10:38 (NRSV) describes "how God anointed Jesus of Nazareth with the Holy Spirit and with power; how he went about doing good and healing all who were oppressed by the devil, for God was with him." Dunn writes that "Jesus was presented as a man inspired by God, as one whose secret of success was the outworking of divine power through him, or, which is the same thing, whose secret of success was that 'God was with him.'"[28] Christ is our example for living by Godly principles and operating in a Spirit-led life and kingdom ministry. Since we are both human and participants of God's divine nature, we have the capacity, through the Holy Spirit, to function from the *charisms* and *dunamis* of the Spirit (cf. Acts 1:8).

The Holy Spirit facilitates communication for the believer with God; thus, believers, out of intimacy and love for God, can simply obey and follow God as sons and daughters of the kingdom (cf. Rom. 8:14). The believer is empowered by the Spirit to do the ministry that Jesus did; this is normative and flows from communion with God. Ruthven states of the Spirit, "It is clear from Scripture that the essence of the New Covenant is the presence of the communicating, prophetic Spirit in our heart (Is 59:21; Acts 2:39; Jer 31:33; 2 Cor 3; Heb 8–12)."[29] Christians, through our union with the divine nature and empowerment of the Spirit, have the potential and capability to do the same miraculous works that Christ performed while on earth. Believers have the same potential and

---

28 Dunn, *Christology*, 138. Dunn continues, "That this too is an ancient evangelistic formulation is made probable by the primitiveness of the title used for Jesus ('Jesus, him from Nazareth') and the indications that behind the passage lie primitive exegetical traditions using particularly Ps 107.20 but also Is 61.1.

29 Ruthven, *What's Wrong*, 125.

capability to perform miraculous works foretold by Christ through the indwelling nature of the Spirit—this should be expected and should be normative for Christians and the church (cf. Jn 14:12; Acts 1:8).

Jürgen Moltmann, theologian and professor emeritus of Systematic Theology at the University of Tübingen, emphasizes that the mission of Jesus is wholly pneumatological. Patrick Oden, assistant professor of Theology and Philosophy at Azusa Pacific University, states of Moltmann's pneumatological view of the mission of Jesus, "The indwelling of the Spirit brings the divine energies of life in Jesus to rapturous and overflowing fullness... the Spirit makes Jesus 'the kingdom of God in person,' for in the power of the Spirit he drives out demons and heals the sick; in the power of the Spirit he receives sinners, and brings the kingdom of God to the poor."[30] Oden continues regarding Moltmann's view of Jesus, "This is the mission that Jesus claimed in Lk 4:18–19, and the mission which the Spirit of the Lord binds upon all those who follow Jesus."[31] According to Ruthven, the phrase "the Spirit of the Lord is upon me" defines the very mission of Christ: "'Spirit' is not emphasizing the Trinity or enthusiasm, but revelation & power (the ministry of a 'prophet mighty in deed & word'—Lk 24:19; Rom 15:18–19) because He has anointed me equates to commissioned to be a prophet /priest/king to preach (announce) good news (gospel)."[32]

---

30 Jürgen Moltmann, *The Spirit of Life*, trans. Margaret Kohl (Minneapolis: Fortress Press, 1992), 61, quoted in Patrick Oden, "An Emerging Pneumatology: Jürgen Moltmann and the Emerging Church in Conversation," *Journal of Pentecostal Theology* 18 (2009): 269.

31 Jürgen Moltmann, *Jesus Christ for Today's World*, trans. Margaret Kohl (Minneapolis: Fortress Press, 1994), 15, quoted in Oden, "An Emerging Pneumatology," 269.

32 Ruthven, DMin Cohort Notes, 11.

Viewing Jesus as the bearer of the Holy Spirit leads to an understanding by Walter Kasper, a German cardinal of the Roman Catholic Church, that "Christ's real identity can only be accounted for in terms of unprecedented relationship to the Spirit."[33] Kasper argues for a "pneumatologically oriented Christology" and asserts that "the same Spirit who permeated the life of Jesus is now made available to others, in order that they might share the same inner life of God."[34] "This Spirit," according to Kasper, "is the life giving power of the creator, who inaugurates the eschatological age of healing and hope."[35] Kasper views the believer as endued with the very Spirit of God and sharing in the same life and nature of God. One could conclude that just as the believer shares in the same inner life and nature of God through Christ, the believer should share in the inaugurated eschatological age of healing and hope through Christ presently.

Ruthven sees an emerging emphasis on Spirit Christology: "The recent trend toward a more biblical 'Spirit Christology' strengthens our thesis that a central NT theme in Jesus' ministry was that he presented not only a unique sacrifice for sin, but as [sic] a normative exemplar of charismatic ministry for others to replicate."[36] Ruthven, using a kenotic emphasis, defines Spirit Christology as "Jesus-as-prototype," stating that Jesus "derives his power and ministry, not from his status as God, as traditional theology would have it, but from the anointing of the Spirit....Jesus' own empowering by the Spirit extends in time into his exaltation, and into the experience of those replicating his life—his disciples."[37] Spirit Christology views the pneumatological role of the Holy Spirit in

33 McGrath, *Christian Theology*, 290.
34 Ibid.
35 Ibid.
36 Ruthven, *What's Wrong*, 238.
37 Ibid., 222. Cf. footnote on this page.

the life of Jesus as inseparable from his Christological nature and function.

According to Pinnock, "When I refer to Spirit Christology, I do so in an orthodox way that preserves the trinitarian distinctions. Spirit Christology enriches but does not replace Logos Christology. It enriches Logos Christology by doing greater justice to the role of Spirit in Christ. It gives better recognition to the missions of both the Son and the Spirit. It neither exaggerates nor diminishes the role of either Person."[38] Pinnock goes on to say that "Logos Christology is ontologically focused, while a Spirit Christology is functionally focused, but the two work together. Generally speaking, Logos addresses the Person of Jesus while Spirit addresses his work."[39] Steven M. Studebaker, associate professor of Systematic and Historical Theology at McMaster Divinity College, states of Pinnock's Spirit Christology, "Spirit Christology brings Christology into a Trinitarian focus. The incarnation is the result of the activity of the Trinitarian God. The Son is incarnated, but the Father and Spirit are involved in the process that constitutes the incarnation of the Son in Jesus Christ."[40] Spirit Christology perhaps best expresses the essence of the Holy Spirit's interaction and anointing upon Jesus Christ—more so than Logos Christology, which tends to be one-sided, as Studebaker states:

> The benefit of Spirit Christology is that it better reflects the biblical data than does the one-sided emphasis of Logos Christology. The Old Testament defines the coming Messiah in terms of pneumatology (Is 11:2; 42:1; and 61:1).

---

38 Pinnock, *Flame of Love*, 92. Cf. Pinnock, *Flame of Love*, 91, "The deity of Christ is seen only in his humanity as filled by the Spirit, and the incarnation is viewed only on the redemptive-historical plane."

39 Ibid., 91.

40 Steven M. Studebaker, "Integrating Pneumatology and Christology: A Trinitarian Modification of Clark H. Pinnock's Spirit Christology," *PNEUMA: The Journal of the Society for Pentecostal Studies,* 28, no. 1 (2006): 9.

The New Testament presents Jesus Christ fulfilling these expectations. Luke 1:35 and Matthew 1:18–20 portray the Spirit bringing about the incarnation. The activity of the Holy Spirit characterizes the life and ministry of Jesus: the Spirit descends on him at his baptism (Mk 1:9–13; Mt 3:13–17; Lk 3:21–22; and Jn 1:32–34), leads him into the wilderness and helps him to overcome temptation (Mk 1:12–13; Mt 4:1–11; and Lk 4:1–3), and resurrects him (Rom 8:9–11). Jesus' consciousness of being Messiah was in terms of bearing the Spirit in a unique fashion (Lk 4:14–21). The early Christians understood Jesus Christ's ministry as a product of the Holy Spirit's presence (Acts 10:38).[41]

It is the very "anointing" by the Holy Spirit that makes Jesus the "Christ" or anointed one. The Holy Spirit is, as Augustine referred to, the "bond of love," who binds God and the Son through eternity and who bound the earthly Jesus to God while he was fulfilling his eschatological mission.[42] Paul writes in Phil 2:7 of Christ coming to earth in human flesh and emptying himself, alluding to a limitation of divine attributes and prerogatives while on earth. In this kenotic passage, Paul gives the reader an indication of Christ's self-imposed divine limitations and dependence upon the Spirit. Likewise, in John's gospel, we read of the dependence that Jesus had upon the Holy Spirit and upon God. John 5:19–20, 30 (NRSV) says "the Son can do nothing on his own." Dunn emphasizes this concept by stating, "Jesus is presented consistently as a man of the Spirit during his life and ministry; not as one who could freely dispense the Spirit."[43] And in Acts 10:38, Peter confirms that it was

---

41 Studebaker, "Integrating," 8.
42 Ibid.
43 Dunn, *Christology*, 141.

the anointing of God that empowered Christ to heal and deliver the oppressed. The result is that Jesus, Emmanuel, performed the works he did as both God and man, dependent upon God the Holy Spirit.

In so doing, Jesus gave the believer a model to emulate, and stated this in Jn 14:12 (NRSV): "Very truly, I tell you, the one who believes in me will also do the works that I do and, in fact, will do greater works than these because I am going to the Father." Upon new birth, the Holy Spirit regenerates the human spirit and enables the believer to function in the *charisms* of the Spirit to reproduce the works of Christ. The believer becomes a partaker of God's divine nature, dependent upon the Holy Spirit as Jesus was, to heal the sick, deliver the oppressed, and minister in the gifts of the Spirit. It is important to note that this empowerment by the Spirit is received and realized through faith and obedience by the believer. The potential for the believer to operate in the *charisms* is resident through the Holy Spirit; however, ignorance and unbelief can render inoperative that which God has freely given.

If Jesus depended upon the Holy Spirit to live life and to minister, how much more should we as believers, individually and corporately, depend upon the Spirit within us to lead, guide, and empower us in our walk with God? In a similar manner, as God sent Jesus, who was empowered by the Spirit to perform his mission, so we have been sent by God and empowered by the Spirit. Pinnock points out that "while Logos Christology highlights how different we are from Jesus, Spirit Christology underlines how like him we can be."[44] While our mission is similar, it certainly is not equal with the mission of Christ. He was God in human flesh, sent to redeem us to God. We have God's nature and anointing by the Spirit to replicate the mission of Christ, but we are not equal

---

44 Pinnock, *Flame of Love*, 111.

with God. In defining the nature of the church, Jason E. Vickers writes, "From its inception, the church has been and is a charismatic community whose life depends entirely on the presence and power of the Holy Spirit, through whom and by whom the church does everything that she does."[45] Pinnock states, "Spirit, who maintained Jesus' relationship with the Father and empowered him for mission, now calls the church into that relationship, giving it the power to carry on the mission."[46] The twenty-first-century church, awakened and renewed to a dependence upon the Spirit and a normative charismatic lifestyle, has the potential to impact modern society on a monumental scale.

Beginning in the twentieth century, a renewal toward a more kerygmatic position of Christology emerged, evident in the writings of Barth and Bultmann. According to McGrath, Barth believed "the church is the community which comes into being in response to the proclamation of the word of God.... Although it would not be correct to say that Barth has a 'charismatic' understanding of the church, his Christological approach to the identity of the church allocates a definite and distinctive role to the Holy Spirit."[47] Barth's ecclesiology included a view of Christology that embraced the Holy Spirit's work in the church, thus causing the church to be seen as an "event" and not an "institution."[48] Rudolf Bultmann, a twentieth-century German Lutheran theologian and professor of New Testament at the University of Marburg, stated, "The word of God is not a statement of abstract truths, but a proclamation."[49]

---

45 Jason E. Vickers, *Minding the Good Ground: A Theology for Church Renewal* (Waco, TX: Baylor University Press, 2011), 36.

46 Pinnock, *Flame of Love*, 114.

47 McGrath, *Christian Theology*, 387.

48 Ibid.

49 Ibid.

While neither of these theologians viewed the proclamation of the word as accompanied by the *charisms*, a renewed kerygmatic emphasis upon the proclamation of the kingdom, not just in word but in a demonstration of power (1 Cor 4:20), has similarities with early church Christology and more modern Spirit Christology. After all, Jesus himself linked a *kerygma* of the kingdom with healing and deliverance of the oppressed, and his very life and message was one of power. Kittel, Friedrich, and Bromiley write, "The message carries with it the fulfillment. The works of Jesus are signs of the messianic age. At Nazareth Jesus applies Is. 61:1 to himself (Lk 4:18). With him the good news of God's kingdom is preached (Lk 16:16). Lk 8:1 sums up the entire ministry of Jesus when it calls him a herald and messenger of the kingdom. His whole life proclaims the gospel." [50]

The historical view of Jesus, which leans upon reason and a philosophical approach to the nature of Christ, and the kerygmatic Christ, who is appropriated by faith, traditionally have created a dichotomy between faith and reason.[51] Millard J. Erickson, professor of Theology at Western Seminary, states in his *Christian Theology*, "Christology from above was the basic strategy and orientation of the Christology of the earliest centuries of the church. It also was, to a large extent, the Christology of orthodoxy during the precritical era when there was no question as to the historical reliability of the whole of Scripture."[52] Emil Brunner, a twentieth-century Swiss Protestant (Reformed) theologian, describes this tension between the historical observation of Christ and the understanding of his nature derived by faith, saying that "Christian

---

50 Kittel, Friedrich, and Bromiley, *Theological Dictionary–Abridged*, 268. Cf. Lk 4:17–21; Is 61:1–2.

51 Millard J. Erickson, *Christian Theology* (Grand Rapids, MI: Baker Books, 2003), 682–691.

52 Ibid., 682.

faith springs only out of the witness to Christ of the preached message and the written word of the Scriptures. The historical picture is indeed included in the latter...; but this picture itself is not the basis of knowledge."[53] The early church clearly saw its role as herald and witness to the good news of Christ, not merely from a historical or critical context, but in bold proclamation of the reality of the resurrection of Jesus through signs following, namely, healing and deliverance.

The kerygmatic Christ and gospel of the early church and church history are ones of word accompanied by power. As Paul explained in 1 Cor 4:20 (NRSV), "For the kingdom of God depends not on talk but on power." Ruthven states, "The nature of the Kingdom is expressed in the typical way God reveals himself: in divine power (1 Cor 2:4–5; 4:19–20). [54] Accordingly, true Christian 'preaching' (presenting the Kingdom) is necessarily expressed in *dunamis* (miracle power Rom 15:19; 2 Cor 12:12; 1 Thes 1:5; 1 Pt 4:6). Through the indwelling nature and anointing of the Holy Spirit in and upon the life of the believer, the *dunamis* of the Spirit is affected to realize a kerygmatic Christ of power. By necessity then, a kerygmatic Christology has pneumatological implications as all proclamations of Christ are Spirit led and empowered (cf. Jn 16:5–15). Furthermore, proclaiming the gospel of the kingdom should be accompanied by signs following, which can only occur by the power of the Spirit (cf. Mk 16:15–20).

---

53 Emil Brunner, *The Mediator* (London: Lutterworth, 1934), 158, quoted in Erickson, *Christian Theology*, 682.

54 Ruthven, *What's Wrong*, 139. Cf. 1 Cor 2:4–5; Rom 15:18–19.

Chapter 14

SOTERIOLOGY

J ust as Christology is ultimately linked and shaped by Christ, we could safely deduce that soteriology is similarly framed by Jesus Christ.[1] The believer's salvation can only be understood accurately in Christ's life, death, and resurrection.[2] Barth referred to soteriology as the "heart of the Church's dogmatics" and Tillich said it is "the heart of every Christian theology."[3] While much of Reformation theology focused upon justification, the essence of New Testament soteriology is one that not only justifies, but transforms us into the likeness and nature of Christ and causes us to share in God's divine life presently. It is in Christ, empowered by the Spirit, that believers are being conformed into his image and the very essence of salvation, which is concurrently past, present, and future, unfolds. Our present realization of salvation includes sharing in the benefits of what the atonement made available to us: justification and freedom from sin, healing for our person and body, and deliverance from demonic oppression.

---

1 McGrath, *Christian Theology*, 318.

2 Ibid., 316.

3 Thomas and Wondra, *Introduction to Theology*, 179.

In looking at the life of Christ through the Gospels, one should see that Christ was just as concerned about salvation for the individual in terms of healing and deliverance as he was about eternal life. Therefore, to understand the believer's salvation apart from the depth of *sōtēria,* which includes healing and deliverance presently, limits the fullness of redemption acquired in Christ. When Paul's writings are examined, we see soteriology in terms of justification, sanctification, and salvation, all of which can be seen with past, present, and future characteristics.[4] Traditional Protestant theology typically defines *salvation* in terms of forgiveness of sins and deliverance from hell; however, as Ruthven states, "Almost all of the references to 'salvation' (Greek: *sōtēria*) in the Gospels are immediately about healing or deliverance. In the rest of the NT, the term can be more general, including eternal salvation. In the NT, 'salvation' includes the whole person in the present as well as the future. Traditional theology stresses 'salvation' from sin and hell."[5] The New Testament provides a broader soteriological context, which includes healing and deliverance, than is found in traditional evangelicalism.

It is important to understand soteriology from a perspective that Christ doesn't just reveal something important to us about salvation; rather, he achieves something for Christians that would not be possible apart from his atonement. As Andrew Sung Park explains, "We are not dealing with the event that happened two thousand years ago alone. The living Jesus and the Paraclete are presently working for our atonement."[6] Park continues, "Jesus' atonement is not his work alone, but his cooperation with God and

---

4 McGrath, *Christian Theology,* 319.

5 Ruthven, DMin Cohort Notes, 16.

6 Andrew Sung Park, *Triune Atonement: Christ's Healing for Sinners, Victims, and the Whole Creation* (Louisville, KY: Westminster John Knox Press, 2009), xi.

the Holy Spirit."[7] This present working of the atonement of Christ and of the Holy Spirit includes our healing both presently and eschatologically. We are saved and are being saved, and the fullness of salvation is yet to be realized. Therefore, we should expect salvation (*sōtēria*) presently to include justification and forgiveness of sin, healing from sickness and disease, and deliverance from demonic oppression.

In discussing soteriology, one atonement model does not completely encapsulate the totality of Christ's salvation. There are benefits in examining the strengths of the various atonement theories to comprise a balanced soteriological view.[8] However, there is one model that warrants a renewed focus by the postmodern church, Christ the victor (*Christus victor*) theory. Referred to by some as the "classical atonement theory," the "Christ the victor" view has significant theological elements that interact and affect the ministry of healing and deliverance.

Kelsey states, "Through the crucifixion and resurrection of Jesus, the power of 'death' (the Evil One) was defeated, so that by following Jesus' way people could be saved from both immoral living and from psychological and physical sickness. The early church knew these forces which Christ defeated."[9] Paul, John, and other writers of the New Testament define the totality of the victory that Christ achieved over the powers of darkness (cf. Eph 6:12; Col 2:15; 1 Jn 3:8). Christ himself in the Great Commission of Matthew 28 stated that all authority had been given to him, implying that by virtue of his death and resurrection, he held the authority over the powers of darkness. He now was delegating his authority to his church and asking them to use what they had been taught to make

---

7 Park, *Triune Atonement*, vi.

8 Cf. Park, *Triune Atonement*, *passim*; Thomas and Wondra, *Introduction to Theology*, 179–183, for a thorough examination of atonement theories.

9 Kelsey, *Healing and Christianity*, 115.

disciples. This involved proclaiming the gospel and demonstrating the kingdom (i.e., exercising their authority in Christ over the stripped-away powers of darkness).

In his treatise *Against Heresies*, Irenaeus describes the normality of healing and deliverance in the church, which is the result of enforcing the victory of Christ over the powers of darkness that cause sickness and demonization. Irenaeus writes, "His disciples receiving grace from Him do in His name perform miracles so as to promote the welfare of other men according to the gift which each one has received from Him....And what shall I more say? It is not possible to name the number of the gifts which the church scattered throughout the whole world has received from God in the name of Jesus Christ."[10]

The early church saw itself in a struggle against the powers of darkness and that sickness, disease, and demonic oppression were primarily the result of evil afflicting humanity. Through the victory of Christ and the authority he imparted to his church, church members viewed themselves as both authorized and commanded to enforce his victory by healing the sick, casting out demons, and setting at liberty those who were oppressed. This was normative Christianity in the early centuries of the church, and a victorious atonement was prevalent in its theology and ministry practice.

Gustaf Aulen, a twentieth-century Bishop of Strängnäs in the Church of Sweden and theologian, in his defining work, *Christus Victor*, reintroduced this earlier church model of atonement of Christ as victor. According to McGrath, Aulen argued that "The classical Christian conception of the work of Christ was summed

---

10 Irenaeus, 2.32.4. Irenaeus continues, "For some do certainly and truly drive out devils so that those who have thus been cleansed from evil spirits frequently both believe in Christ and join themselves to the church. Others have foreknowledge of things to come they see visions and utter prophetic expressions. Others still heal the sick by laying their hands upon them and they are made whole. Yea moreover as I have said the dead even have been raised up and remained among us for many years."

up in the belief that the risen Christ had brought new possibilities of life to humanity through his victory over the powers of evil."[11] Aulen believed this atonement theory was the "classical" approach to the atonement through the Middle Ages.[12] Park states concerning Aulen's *Christus Victor* atonement theory, "He believed that this idea was upheld by the NT and the early church. Consequently, he called it 'the classic idea of atonement.'"[13] McGrath summarizes Aulen's view by stating, "Its central theme is the idea of the Atonement as a divine conflict and victory; Christ—Christus Victor—fights against and triumphs over the evil powers of the world, the 'tyrants' under which mankind is in bondage and suffering, and in Him God reconciles the world to Himself."[14] McGrath further summarizes Aulen's view: "He asserted that this classic idea was reinvigorated by Luther. Under the name of the 'classic idea,' he includes the model of dualistic battles between God and Satan and the model of ransom."[15]

Park lists the strengths of the *Christus Victor* atonement theory: "First, it counts both the death and resurrection of Jesus for our salvation, as does the ransom theory. Second, it acknowledges our struggle against some forces of evil beyond human sins: the rulers, the authorities, and the cosmic powers of this present darkness (Eph 6:12). Third, it realistically describes our daily struggles with the power of evil."[16]

A fourth point, which I believe could be added to Park's summary, would be the authority of the believer over the powers of darkness through the victory of Christ and infilling of the Holy

---

11 McGrath, *Christian Theology*, 324.

12 Ibid., 325.

13 Park, *Triune Atonement*, 11.

14 McGrath, *Christian Theology*, 325.

15 Ibid.

16 Park, *Triune Atonement*, 14.

Spirit. This is an essential point, and one the early church understood and openly demonstrated by healing the sick, performing
miracles, and casting out demons. This was normative to the early
church as its members knew they were more than conquerors in
Christ through his resurrection and victory over evil.

During the Enlightenment, the church moved away from the
view of *Christus Victor*, demythologizing Satan and demonic forces.[17]
The rationalistic approach to salvation during the Enlightenment
minimized the power of the cross and the authority given to the
church to advance the kingdom of God through the works of the
Spirit (i.e., healing, deliverance, miracles, etc.). While this *Christus
Victor* view seemed "outdated" to many during this period, and still
seems so for many today, the reality is that Satan and his cohorts,
although stripped of their authority through Christ (cf. Col 2:15),
are very much present and active in our world (cf. Eph 6:12) until
the full consummation of God's kingdom at the return of Christ.
It is imperative for believers to know their authority in Christ and
how to enforce his victory against the powers of darkness to heal
the sick, liberate the oppressed, and advance the church and kingdom in our time.

---

17 McGrath, *Christian Theology*, 324.

Chapter 15

CONCLUSION

We have examined a healing theme in both the Old and New Testaments. God is a healer, establishing this truth early in Hebrew thought and practice. Christ's atonement was vicarious for both sin and sickness; therefore, salvation and healing are available today through the finished work of the cross. The missional work of Jesus, demonstrating the gospel of the kingdom of God in power, was to be replicated by disciples of all ages until his return. Salvation, healing, and deliverance should be normative in the missional life of the church presently.

The life and ministry of Jesus Christ demonstrated his divinity, his humanity, and his dependence upon the Holy Spirit. A Christology apart from a pneumatological relationship seems contrary to the very function of the Trinity while Christ was incarnate. A form of Spirit Christology, which envelops a functional view of Christ and his mission and ministry while on earth, is a more biblical approach to Christology. As a result of his reliance upon the Spirit, Christ gave his followers an example of how to live dependent upon and empowered by the Holy Spirit. He demonstrated that this relationship with the Holy Spirit was necessary to live a fruitful life and to function dynamically in ministry. The very proclamation of Christ and the kingdom of God should demonstrate the power of the kingdom, through healing and deliverance, not just oral communication and intellectual reasoning.

Understanding that Christ is victorious over evil and all powers, and that all authority has been given to him and delegated to the believer in his name, is essential to walking in the authority that God intended. There simply is no substitute for advancing the kingdom of God apart from a soteriological view that is victorious, because its perspective is rooted in the victory of Jesus. Christ commissioned, gave authority, and by the Holy Spirit, empowered those who would believe and follow him to do the works that he did, namely, to heal the sick, cast out demons, and even raise the dead (cf. Mt 10:7, 8; 28:18–20; Jn 14:12). A theology and kingdom ministry model of power should be normative for believers, and when practiced, the ministry of healing and deliverance, as well as all of the *charisms*, is still operative and effective in our twenty-first century.

The rapid growth of the church during the Patristic period, by some estimates as many as a half a million converts in each generation, was primarily a consequence of believers in Jesus Christ continuing his kingdom ministry model in Roman culture.[1] They were unrelenting in healing the sick, casting out demons, and operating in the gifts of the Spirit. Through kingdom discipleship models, they in turn taught others, who continued this ministry and repeated the cycle of discipleship training and ministry.

By the end of the Patristic period, a shift away from the common practice of healing and deliverance ministry was occurring. As previously stated, Augustine in his earlier writings declared that Christians should not look to a continuance of healing and

---

1 MacMullen, *Christianizing the Roman Empire*, 110.

deliverance ministry. While Augustine changed his views concerning healing shortly before his death, the Christian culture was changing, and most Christians were no longer en masse ministering in healing, but this did not nullify the truth that God was still healing through the prayers of his people who understood this.

As Christianity progressed into the Middle Ages, healing and deliverance ministry was primarily the work of ascetic monks. Rarely, at least in the recorded histories, was the ordinary believer operating in the power of the *charisms*, nor did Christians have a theological framework for healing and deliverance ministry as normative in Christian culture. Church leaders, like Pope Gregory the Great, believed in healings and miracles, but believed these were the exception, not the rule, for the typical Christian. These graces were relegated to a few chosen saints who could perform the cures and miracles.

Furthermore, there was a theological shift away from sickness and disease being considered the work of the devil and something that the victory of Christ came to abolish. In its place, the belief that sickness and disease were associated with the will of God, God permitting sickness and suffering to punish us for sin and to draw us near to him, became the prevailing theological belief. The result was that faith for healing largely disappeared. After all, if God has brought the sickness, and if it is God's will for a person to be sick, then one must simply accept the will of God and suffer or die. If it is God's will for a person to be healed, then he or she may be healed. Additionally, an emphasis on being prepared for eternal life became more of a focus. Instead of anointing with oil to heal the sick, now the church anointed the sick in preparation of death.

Aquinas and his theology, largely influenced by Greek philosopher Aristotle, greatly hindered the ministry of healing and deliverance in the church. Sacramental healing and experience in the

Spirit gave way to reason, argument, and an emphasis on doctrine and teaching. Aquinas and most of the Reformers saw healing and miracles as necessary for the confirmation of the divinity of Christ and the Christian message, but believed that now these truths were established, the ministry of healing and deliverance by Christians was no longer needed.

During the Reformation, healings and miracles became part of the contentious issues between the Reformers and the Catholic Church. The Catholic Church, in attempting to discredit and invalidate the Reformers and their diverging theological views, essentially challenged the Reformers regarding the lack of miracles in their movement. The Reformers, largely led by Calvin, determined that the purpose of miracles was to confirm the divinity of Christ and confirm the gospel witness. Once true doctrine (according to the Reformers) was established, the need for the continuation of the *charisms* was no longer necessary. Consequently the faith, belief, and practice of healing and deliverance ministry in both the Catholic and Protestant church were diminished significantly. Kelsey succinctly states this distressing theological position of many in the church regarding healing and miracles: "The church speaks of miracles as if they were a public exhibition once staged, but ignores the desire of an incredibly compassionate God to reach out to human beings here and now in transforming experiences of grace and healing."[2]

Despite the gifts of healing and deliverance ministry being predominately disregarded and viewed as no longer relevant for the church, God has continued to maintain a remnant of believers throughout the church age who have believed and practiced healing and deliverance with effective results. Kelsey writes,

---

2 Kelsey, *Healing and Christianity*, 176.

It is also clear that the people whom Jesus sent out to heal understood this ministry in a way that is as relevant to our lives today as it was then. If the same Spirit is in the church today as in that time, then the same things can happen once again. Unless one dismisses the entire record of healings as fiction, or restricts it by a framework such as dispensationalism, no other conclusion is possible. We must acknowledge that a major part of the gospel account is devoted to healings.[3]

Gordon observes that miracles have been the standard throughout every revival and reformation of the church:

But now comes a most suggestive fact: that whenever we find a revival of primitive faith and apostolic simplicity, there we find a profession of the chaste and evangelical miracles which characterized the apostolic age. These attend the cradle of every spiritual reformation, as they did the birth of the Church herself. Waldenses, Moravians, Huguenots, Covenanters, Friends, Baptists and Methodists all have their record of them.[4]

Keener concludes, "Miracle claims, especially regarding healings, are by Western standards surprisingly common (though by no means universal) in regions of the world where such events are expected. These claims include, as in the Gospels and Acts, the healing of the blind, those unable to walk, and the raising of the dead, among many others."[5] As he points out, the sheer number and frequency of global reports of healings and miracles, while

---

3 Kelsey, *Healing and Christianity*, 101.
4 Gordon, "Ministry of Healing," 159.
5 Keener, *Miracles*, 2:761.

all cannot be verified or proven, attest to the ongoing, present-day *charism* of healing in the church.[6]

The Pentecostal and Charismatic churches have continued to grow at a momentous rate since the beginning of the twentieth century due principally to the practice of this kingdom ministry model taught and demonstrated by Christ and passed on to successive disciples through the centuries. Candy Gunther Brown states, "Divine healing practices are an essential marker of Pentecostal and Charismatic Christianity as a global phenomenon."[7] Today, Pentecostal and Charismatic Christians are the largest sector within Protestantism, demographers estimating nearly six hundred million in 2006 and potentially one billion by 2040.[8] Ruthven writes, "This Pentecostal, or charismatic, movement has emerged as the largest branch of Protestantism, even perhaps the largest active branch of Christianity, with estimates ranging to over 700 million adherents world-wide."[9] Luis Lugo states, "According to the Pew Forum on Religion and Public Life's *Spirit and Power: A 10-Country Survey of Pentecostals* (2006), more than a quarter—and in many countries two-thirds—of the world's two billion Christians identify themselves as Pentecostal or Charismatic."[10]

Similar to the early church, the continued growth of this segment of Christianity is primarily due to the belief, faith, and practice of the *charisms* of the Spirit, specifically relating to healing and deliverance ministry as practiced by Christ and his disciples. Amanda Porterfield states, "Much as Christianity succeeded during its first centuries as a relatively effective form of health care,

---

6 Keener, *Miracles*, 2:761.

7 Brown, *Global*, 3.

8 Lederle, *Theology with Spirit*, 2.

9 Ruthven, *Cessation*, 2.

10 Luis Lugo, *Spirit and Power: A 10-Country Survey of Pentecostals* (Washington, DC: Pew Forum on Religion and Public Life, Oct. 2006), quoted in Brown, *Global*, 3.

Pentecostalism succeeds today for some of the same reasons. And much as Christianity's effectiveness as a healing cult facilitated its spread throughout the far-flung Roman Empire in late antiquity, healing performances enable Pentecostalism to grow in many parts of the early twenty-first century world."[11] In writing about the international ministry of Global Awakening and its contribution toward the global expansion of Christianity, Brown states, "By emphasizing the capacity of 'ordinary' Christians as agents of healing, North American Pentecostals facilitate the democratization of global healing practices. In turn, supernaturalizing trends return to North America through people's exposure to worldviews and rituals in such places as Brazil and Mozambique."[12]

Truly, "Jesus Christ is the same yesterday and today and forever" (Heb 13:8 NRSV). God continues to use ordinary disciples, trained in the mission and ministry of Christ, to bring God's kingdom to earth through the ongoing *charisms* of the Spirit, that the world may know God's love and compassion and taste of the fullness of God's kingdom to come. Greig writes, "Nowhere does Scripture teach that the miraculous healing ministry and spiritual gifts exercised by Jesus, the apostles, and the laity of the Early Church are not to be continued today. Jas 5:14–16 quite clearly suggests the contrary, as well as Rom 12:6–8; 1 Cor 12:7–11, 28–30; 14:22–39; Gal 3:5; Phil 4:9 (and 1 Cor 11:1); 1 Thes 5:19–21; 2 Tm 1:6; and 1 Pt 4:10, 11."[13] The themes of healing, deliverance, miracles, and *charisms* of the Spirit have continued since Christ, and history well records this reality.[14]

---

11 Porterfield, *Healing*, 174.
12 Brown, *Global*, 353.
13 Greig, "The Purpose of Signs," 163.
14 E-mail to author on October 6, 2014 from Ruthven: "The core of Pauline theology could not possibly be more explicit about the universal continuation of the charismata such as prophecy and healing: 'It is the same God who energizes all [all the

The argument and case for the continuance of the gifts of the Spirit in our day, which include healing and deliverance, are convincing and essential for the church to walk in the fullness of the mission Christ gave the church. My journey began as a young believer with little knowledge or understanding of this important subject. Now, nearly thirty years later, not only have my understanding and knowledge significantly increased in this subject area, but what I have witnessed by way of healing and deliverance ministry to others, through my life and with other Christians as they minister, has been nothing short of astounding. The testimonies are common at our church, so common that at times when I have people share their testimony of healing to the congregation, I often have to remind the church to celebrate what God has just done!

I recently returned from a missions trip to an unreached people group, in which less than 2 percent of the population were Christian, in the Sonjo region of Tanzania. I preached the first night of an evangelistic crusade in one of the villages, and to start the meeting, I shared with the people testimonies of healings the team had seen earlier that day as we went through the village, as well as other miracles, including the dead being raised in the name of Christ. Then we prayed specifically for those with deaf ears, those who were blind, and those who had back problems. Several people with back problems were healed, two people with deaf ears had their hearing restored, and one person who was totally blind in one eye regained sight—Jesus demonstrated the truth of the gospel of the kingdom by confirming with signs following (Mk 16). Next, I shared and preached about Jesus Christ, how God loved them, died for them, and wanted to heal and bless them—then I invited them to receive Jesus, whom they had just heard about, and

---

charismata] in *everyone.*' (1 Cor 12:6). 'The *charismata* and the calling of God are *not withdrawn!*' (Rom 11:29)."

through the authority of his name and by the power of the Holy Spirit, witness the sick healed through the team. The crowd was between 250 and 300 people, and approximately thirty people gave their lives to Christ that night—most of them, if not all, had never heard about Jesus before this day. That's about 10 percent of the crowd, and the crowd represented about 50 percent of the village population. You may be wondering, "Is this an isolated case?" No, the situations and people groups differ, but I've seen God move in this power in different settings around the world. This is the gospel of the kingdom Jesus asked us to proclaim—one that is not just in word but in power that demonstrates his love, compassion, and power to humanity.

For more testimonies of healing, visit the Passion Church website at www.passiontucson.org. On the website, there are both written testimonies and a link to our YouTube site of video testimonies of healings at our church. My sincere prayer is that you will experience God's healing power as normal in your life and in your church culture. May you have passion for Jesus and compassion for the world—He is the same yesterday, today, and forever!

BIBLIOGRAPHY

Albl, Martin C. "'Are Any among You Sick?' The Health Care System in the Letter of James." *Journal of Biblical Literature* 121, no. 1 (March 1, 2002): 123–143.

Athanasius. *Life of St. Antony.* http://www.newadvent.org/fathers/2811.htm.

———. *On the Incarnation.* http://www.newadvent.org/fathers/2802.htm.

Augustine. *De Vera Religione.* Quoted in Morton Kelsey, *Healing and Christianity: A Classic Study.* Minneapolis, MN: Augsburg Fortress, 1995.

———. *The City of God.* http://www.fordham.edu/halsall/source/augustine-cityofgod-22-9-10.asp.

Bartlett, David L. "The First Letter of Peter: Introduction, Commentary, and Reflections." *The New Interpreter's Bible*, vol. 12, 227–319. Nashville, TN: Abingdon Press, 1998.

Bokovay, W. Kelly. "The Relationship of Physical Healing to the Atonement." *Didaskalia (Otterburne, MB)* 3, no. 1 (October 1, 1991): 24–39.

Boring, M. Eugene. "The Gospel of Matthew: Introduction, Commentary, and Reflections," *The New Interpreter's Bible*, vol. 8, 87–505. Nashville, TN: Abingdon Press, 1995.

———. "1 Peter." In *Abingdon New Testament Commentaries*. Nashville, TN: Abingdon Press, 1999.

Borobio, Dionisio. "An Enquiry into Healing Anointing in the Early Church." *Pastoral Care of the Sick* (1991): 37–49.

Boys, Thomas. *The Suppressed Evidence, or Proofs of the Miraculous Faith and Experince of the Church of Christ in All Ages.* London: Hamilton, Adams & Co., 1832.

Brooke, Avery. "Christian Healing in History." *Weavings* 6 (1991): 6–19.

Brown, Candy Gunther, ed. *Global Pentecostal and Charismatic Healing.* New York: Oxford University Press, 2011.

———. *Testing Prayer: Science and Healing.* Cambridge, MA: Harvard University Press, 2012.

Brown, Francis, Samuel Rolles Driver, and Charles Augustus Briggs, *Enhanced Brown-Driver-Briggs Hebrew and English Lexicon.* Oak Harbor, WA: Logos Research Systems, 2000.

Brown, Michael L. *Israel's Divine Healer.* Grand Rapids, MI: Zondervan Publishing House, 1995.

Brueggemann, Walter. "Healing and its Opponents." In *I Am the Lord Who Heals You,* 1–6. Nashville, TN: Abingdon Press, 2004.

———. "The Book of Exodus: Introduction, Commentary, and Reflections." *The New Interpreter's Bible,* vol. 1, 675–981. Nashville, TN: Abingdon Press, 1994.

Brunner, Emil. *The Mediator.* London: Lutterworth, 1934. Quoted in Millard J. Erickson, *Christian Theology.* Grand Rapids, MI: Baker Books, 2003.

Campbell, Iain D. *Opening Up Exodus.* Leominster, UK: Day One Publications, 2006.

Charles, Archbishop of Glasgow. *The History of St. Cuthbert.* New York: Catholic Publication Society, 1887.

Clark, Randy. *Lighting Fires.* Lake Mary, FL: Creation House, 1998.

———. *There is More!: Reclaiming the Power of Impartation.* Mechanicsburg, PA: Global Awakening, 2006.

Coogan, Michael D., ed. *The New Oxford Annotated Bible: New Revised Standard Version with Apocrypha.* 4th ed. New York: Oxford University Press, 2010.

Cullman, Oscar. *The Christology of the New Testament*. Philadelphia: Westminster Press, 1959.

Curtis, Heather D. "The Global Character of Nineteenth-Century Divine Healing." In *Global Pentecostal and Charismatic Healing*, edited by Candy Gunther Brown. New York: Oxford University Press, 2011.

Cyprian of Carthage, *The Epistles of Cyprian*.

De Arteaga, William L. *Forging a Renewed Hebraic and Pauline Christianity*. Unpublished Manuscript, 2011.

Dunn, James D. G. *Christology in the Making*. London: SCM Press, 1989.

Eire, Carlos. *War against the Idols: The Reformation of Worship from Erasmus to Calvin*. New York: Cambridge University Press, 1986.

Erickson, Millard J. *Christian Theology*. Grand Rapids, MI: Baker Books, 2003.

Eusebius of Caesaria. "Church History." In *A Select Library of the Nicene and Post-Nicene Fathers of the Christian Church, Second Series, Volume I: Eusebius: Church History, Life of Constantine the Great, and Oration in Praise of Constantine*, edited by Philip Schaff and Henry Wace and translated by Arthur Cushman McGiffert. New York: Christian Literature Company, 1890.

Fee, Gordon D. *The Disease of the Health and Wealth Gospels*. Costa Mesa, CA: The Word for Today, 1979. Quoted in Jeffery Niehaus, "Old Testament Foundations: Signs and Wonders in Prophetic Ministry and the Substitutionary Atonement of Isaiah 53." In *The Kingdom and the Power,* edited by Gary S. Grieg and Kevin N. Springer. Ventura, CA: Regal Books, 1993.

Gesenius, Wilhelm, and Samuel Prideaux Tregelles. *Gesenius' Hebrew and Chaldee Lexicon to the Old Testament Scriptures.* Bellingham, WA: Logos Research Systems, 2003.

Gordon, A. J. "The Ministry of Healing." In *Healing: The Three Great Classics on Divine Healing,* edited by Jonathan L. Graf. Camp Hill, PA: Christian Publications, 1992.

Gregory the Great. "Dialogues." In *The Fathers of the Church: A New Translation,* Vol. 39, edited by Odo John Zimmerman. New York: Fathers of the Church, 1959. http://www.archive. org/details/fathersofthechur009513mbp.

———. *Homily on the Gospels.* Quoted in Jon Mark Ruthven, *On the Cessation of the Charismata: The Protestant Polemic on Postbiblical Miracles-Revised and Expanded Edition.* Tulsa, OK: Word & Spirit Press, 2011.

Greig, Gary S., and Catherine B. Greig. "Prayer & Power Evangelism: Learning to Depend on the Holy Spirit, His Healing, His Gifts, & His Power to Follow the Pattern of Jesus' Kingdom Ministry to Spread the Gospel." http://www.cwgministries.org/books/ Power-Evangelism.pdf.

Greig, Gary S. "The Purpose of Signs and Wonders in the New Testament." In *The Kingdom and the Power,* edited by Gary S. Grieg and Kevin N. Springer. Ventura, CA: Regal Books, 1993.

Harrington, Daniel J. *The Gospel of Matthew.* Sacra Pagina 1. Collegeville, MN: The Liturgical Press, 1991. Quoted in Edgar Krentz, "Missionary Matthew: Matthew 28:16–20 as Summary of the Gospel." *Currents In Theology And Mission* 31, no. 1 (2004): 24–31.

Hooker, Morna D. "Mark, The Gospel According to." In *The Oxford Companion to the Bible,* edited by Bruce M. Metzger and Michael D. Coogan. New York: Oxford University Press, 1993.

Hyatt, Eddie L. *2000 Years of Charismatic Christianity: A 21st Century Look at Church History from a Pentecostal/Charismatic Perspective.* Lake Mary, FL: Charisma House, 2002.

Ignatius. *To the Ephesians.* Quoted in Amanda Porterfield, *Healing in the History of Christianity.* New York: Oxford University Press, 2005.

Irenaeus. "Irenæus against Heresies." In *The Ante-Nicene Fathers, Volume I: The Apostolic Fathers With Justin Martyr and Irenaeus,* edited by Alexander Roberts, James Donaldson, and A. Cleveland Coxe. Buffalo, NY: Christian Literature Company, 1885.

———. "Against Heresies." In *Ante-Nicene Christian Library.* Edited by Alexander Roberts and James Donaldson. Edinburg, UK: T. & T. Clark, 1968.

Johnson, Bill, and Randy Clark. *The Essential Guide to Healing: Equipping All Christians to Pray for the Sick.* Bloomington, MN: Chosen Books, 2011.

———. *Healing: Unplugged.* Bloomington, MN: Chosen Books, 2012.

Justin Martyr. "The Second Apology of Justin." In *The Ante-Nicene Fathers, Volume I: The Apostolic Fathers With Justin Martyr and Irenaeus,* edited by Alexander Roberts, James Donaldson, and A. Cleveland Coxe, 190–200. Buffalo, NY: Christian Literature Company, 1885.

Keener, Craig S. *Miracles: The Credibility of the New Testament Accounts,* Vols. 1 and 2. Grand Rapids, MI: Baker Academic, 2011.

Kelber, Werner. *The Oral and the Written Gospel.* Philadelphia: Fortress, 1983. Quoted in Raymond Pickett, "Following Jesus in Galilee: Resurrection as Empowerment in the Gospel of Mark." *Currents in Theology and Missions* 32, no. 6 (2005): 434–444.

Kelsey, Morton. *Healing and Christianity: A Classic Study.* Minneapolis, MN: Augsburg Fortress, 1995.

Kittel, Gerhard, Gerhard Friedrich, and Geoffrey William Bromiley. *Theological Dictionary of the New Testament, Abridged in One Volume.* Grand Rapids, MI: W. B. Eerdmans, 1985.

———. *Theological Dictionary of the New Testament.* 10 vols. Grand Rapids, MI: W. B. Eerdmans, 1964.

Krentz, Edgar. "Missionary Matthew: Matthew 28:16–20 as Summary of the Gospel." *Currents In Theology And Mission* 31, no. 1 (February 1, 2004): 24–31.

Kylstra, Chester, and Betsy Kylstra. *An Integrated Approach to Biblical Healing Ministry.* Tonbridge, UK: Sovereign World, 2003.

Lederle, Henry I. *Theology with Spirit: The Future of the Pentecostal & Charismatic Movements in the Twenty-First Century.* Tulsa, OK: Word & Spirit Press, 2010.

Litwak, Kenneth D. "The Use of Quotations from Isaiah 52:13–53:12 in the New Testament." *Journal of the Evangelical Theological Society* 26, no. 4 (December 1, 1983): 385–394.

Louw, Johannes P., and Eugene Albert Nida. *Greek-English Lexicon of the New Testament: Based on Semantic Domains.* Vols. 1 and 2. New York: United Bible Societies, 1996.

Lugo, Luis. *Spirit and Power: A 10-Country Survey of Pentecostals.* Washington, DC: Pew Forum on Religion and Public Life, 2006. Quoted in Candy Gunther Brown, ed. *Global Pentecostal and Charismatic Healing.* New York: Oxford University Press, 2011.

MacMullen, Ramsey. *Christianizing the Roman Empire (AD 100–400).* New Haven, CT: Yale University, 1984.

Mayhue, Richard L. "For What Did Christ Atone in Isa 53:4–5." *Master's Seminary Journal* 6, no. 2 (1995): 121–141.

McGrath, Alister E. *Christian Theology: An Introduction.* Chichester, UK: Wiley-Blackwell, 2011.

Moltmann, Jürgen. *Jesus Christ for Today's World.* Translated by Margaret Kohl. Minneapolis: Fortress Press, 1994. Quoted in Patrick Oden, "An Emerging Pneumatology: Jürgen Moltmann and the Emerging Church in Conversation." *Journal of Pentecostal Theology* 18 (2009): 263–284.

———. *The Spirit of Life.* Translated by Margaret Kohl. Minneapolis: Fortress Press, 1992. Quoted in Patrick Oden, "An Emerging Pneumatology: Jürgen Moltmann and the Emerging Church in Conversation." *Journal of Pentecostal Theology* 18 (2009): 263–284.

Newport, Kenneth G. C., ed. *The Sermons of Charles Wesley: A Critical Edition and Introduction and Notes.* Oxford, UK: Oxford University Press, 2001. Quoted in Jason E. Vickers, "Charles Wesley's Doctrine of the Holy Spirit: a Vital Resource for the Renewal of Methodism Today." *Asbury Journal* 61, no. 1 (2006): 47–60.

Niehaus, Jeffery. "Old Testament Foundations: Signs and Wonders in Prophetic Ministry and the Substitutionary Atonement of Isaiah 53." In *The Kingdom and the Power,* edited by Gary S. Grieg and Kevin N. Springer. Ventura, CA: Regal Books, 1993.

Oden, Patrick. "An Emerging Pneumatology: Jürgen Moltmann and the Emerging Church in Conversation." *Journal of Pentecostal Theology* 18, no. 2 (2009): 263–284.

Origen, "Origen against Celsus." In *The Ante-Nicene Fathers, Volume IV: Fathers of the Third Century: Tertullian, Part Fourth; Minucius Felix; Commodian; Origen, Parts First and Second,* edited by Alexander Roberts, James Donaldson, and A. Cleveland Coxe, and translated by Frederick Crombie. Buffalo, NY: Christian Literature Company, 1885.

Park, Andrew Sung. *Triune Atonement: Christ's Healing for Sinners, Victims, and the Whole Creation.* Louisville, KY: Westminster John Knox Press, 2009.

Pereira, Matthew J. "The Internal Coherence of Cyril of Alexandria's Pneumatology: Interpreting the 7th Dialogue of the Dialogues on the Trinity." *Union Seminary Quarterly Review* 62, no. 3–4 (2010): 70–98.

Perkins, Pheme. "The Gospel of Mark: Introduction, Commentary, and Reflections." *The New Interpreter's Bible*, vol. 8, 507–733. Nashville, TN: Abingdon Press, 1996.

Pherigo, Lindsey P. "The Gospel According to Mark." In *The Interpreter's One-Volume Commentary on the Bible: Introduction and Commentary for Each Book of the Bible Including the Apocrypha*, edited by Charles M. Laymon, 644–671. Nashville, TN: Abingdon Press, 1971.

Pickett, Raymond. "Following Jesus in Galilee: Resurrection as Empowerment in the Gospel of Mark." *Currents in Theology and Mission* 32, no. 6 (December 1, 2005): 434–444.

Pinnock, Clark H. *Flame of Love: A Theology of the Holy Spirit.* Downers Grove, IL: Inter Varsity Press Academic, 1996.

Porterfield, Amanda. *Healing in the History of Christianity.* New York: Oxford University Press, 2005.

Reichenbach, Bruce R. "By His Stripes We Are Healed." *Journal of the Evangelical Theological Society* 41, no. 4 (1998): 551–560.

Ruthven, Jon Mark. *On the Cessation of the Charismata: The Protestant Polemic on Postbiblical Miracles-Revised and Expanded Edition.* Tulsa, OK: Word & Spirit Press, 2011.

———. *What's Wrong with Protestant Theology?* Unpublished manuscript, 2011.

Senior, Donald. *The Gospel of Matthew, Interpreting Biblical Texts*, 110–177. Nashville, TN: Abingdon Press, 1997.

Sietz, Christopher R. "The Book of Isaiah 40–66: Introduction, Commentary, and Reflection." *The New Interpreter's Bible*, vol. 6, 307–552. Nashville, TN: Abingdon Press, 2001.

Soanes, C., and A. Stevenson. *Concise Oxford English Dictionary*. 11th ed. Oxford, UK: 2004.

Spence-Jones, H. D. M., ed. *Exodus*. The Pulpit Commentary, Vol. 2. London, Funk & Wagnalls Company, 1909.

Stein, Robert H. "The Ending of Mark." *Bulletin for Biblical Research* 18, no. 1 (2008): 79–98.

Strong, James. *A Concise Dictionary of the Words in the Greek Testament and The Hebrew Bible*. Vol. 2. Bellingham, WA: Logos Research Systems, 2009.

Studebaker, Steven M. "Integrating Pneumatology and Christology: A Trinitarian Modification of Clark H. Pinnock's Spirit Christology." *Pneuma* 28, no. 1 (2006): 5–20.

Synan, Vinson. *The Century of the Holy Spirit: 100 Years of Pentecostal and Charismatic Renewal*. Nashville, TN: Thomas Nelson, 2001.

Tertullian, *To Scapula.*

Thomas, Owen C., and Wondra, Ellen K. *Introduction to Theology.* Harrisburg, PA: Morehouse Publishing, 2002.

Thomas, Robert L. *New American Standard Hebrew-Aramaic and Greek Dictionaries.* Anaheim, CA: Foundation Publications, 1998.

Tillich, Paul. *Systematic Theology.* Vol. 2. Chicago: University of Chicago Press, 1951.

Vickers, Jason E. "Charles Wesley's Doctrine of the Holy Spirit: a Vital Resource for the Renewal of Methodism Today." *Asbury Journal* 61, no. 1 (2006): 47–60.

———. "The Making of a Trinitarian Theologian: The Holy Spirit in Charles Wesley's Sermons." *Pneuma* 31 (2009): 213–224.

———. *Minding the Good Ground: A Theology for Church Renewal.* Waco, TX: Baylor University Press, 2011.

Warfield, Benjamin B. *Counterfeit Miracles.* New York: Charles Scribner's Sons, 1918.

Warrington, Keith. "James 5:14–18: Healing Then and Now." *International Review of Mission* 93, no. 370–371 (2004): 346–367.

Waugh, Geoff. *Revival Fires: History's Mighty Revivals.* Mechanicsburg, PA: The Apostolic Network of Global Awakening, 2011.

Wesley, John. *The Works of John Wesley.* Vol. 8. Grand Rapids: MI, Zondervan Publishing House, 1958.

White, William. *Theological Wordbook of the Old Testament*. Edited by R. Laird Harris, Gleason L. Archer, Jr., and Bruce K. Waltke. Chicago: Moody Press, 1999.

Wimber, John, and Kevin Springer. *Power Evangelism*. Ventura, CA: Regal, 2009.

———. *Power Healing*. New York: HarperCollins, 1987.

Young, Brad H. *Jesus the Jewish Theologian*. Peabody, MA: Hendrickson Publishers, 1995.

Made in the USA
Lexington, KY
08 March 2016